THE FIRST SARATOGA

The First
Saratoga

*Being the Saga of John Young
and His Sloop-of-War*

By

WILLIAM BELL CLARK

LOUISIANA STATE UNIVERSITY PRESS
Baton Rouge

MANUFACTURED IN THE UNITED STATES OF AMERICA
BY THE WILLIAM BYRD PRESS, INC.,
RICHMOND, VIRGINIA

Preface

THIS is the story of a man and a ship—a gallant sea captain whose deeds have passed into oblivion; a stanch sloop-of-war that plied the seas for three brief, sensational cruises and then, like her commander, entered the limbo of the forgotten. The man was John Young, one-time shipmaster of New York and later twenty-third captain in order of seniority in the navy of the American Revolution. The ship was the Continental sloop-of-war *Saratoga,* which, somewhere in the latitude of the Bahamas, started for the American navy that sad list to which many a fighting craft has been added since: "Lost at sea, unheard of."

There are many who figure prominently in this tale —among them Joanna Young, the devoted wife of the captain, and Francis Lewis, one of New York's great Revolutionary figures. And there are other naval vessels which appear: the *Trumbull,* the *Deane,* and the *Confederacy,* to mention a few. Primarily, however, this is the saga of John Young and the *Saratoga.*

Some naval officers of the American Revolution deserve the honor history has accorded them. Others have attained celebrity of a sort through eulogistic biographers rather than by demonstrated merit. Still others, worthy of fame but neglected by historians and lacking advocates, have been relegated to obscurity.

As an exemplar of the gallant group of the unappreciated stands John Young. Passing reference to him may be found in a few histories and biographies. He has been called James Young, J. Young, Captain Young, but seldom his proper Christian name. So what value such mention? Net profit either to history or to John Young's reputation has been negligible.

Justice to him with its corollary—better light upon certain naval phases of the American Revolution—involves more than "unscrambling" the few historical facts so far printed. Papers bearing upon this virtually unknown naval officer are available in many domestic and foreign archives. To consult them, to separate fact from fallacy, to arrive at an adequate portrayal of John Young has been a fascinating experience. It might be likened to an intricate jig-saw puzzle with a few pieces put together and the bulk of them missing. As lost parts were located, it was apparent that the original pieces had been misfitted by those playing with them in the past. Pieces are still missing, but enough have been found to appreciate the picture.

Once assembled, John Young emerges—capable, daring, resourceful, hot-tempered—a participant in many hitherto unrecorded and picturesque episodes of the naval war, a sea-fighter whose brilliant victories enhance the annals of the American navy. We find this Continental captain who has been neglected by history contributing most meritorious services to the infant United States. We discover a career replete with interest from the time he landed a gunpowder cargo in 1776 until, four years later, he and his little sloop-of-war *Saratoga* vanished at sea.

\ John Young was a protégé of Francis Lewis. He

was a confidant of John Paul Jones and shared with
Jones the honor of receiving the first official salute
given by a foreign power to the Stars and Stripes. He
was trusted and appreciated by that indefatigable
miracle-worker Robert Morris. Twice during his naval
activities he rendered signal services to George Washington. Add to that his acquaintanceship with Henry
Laurens, William Livingston, and William Ellery,
and his intimate association with John Barry, Seth
Harding, and James, John, and Samuel Nicholson,
and other Continental naval captains, and we see that
John Young moved in a sphere of no mean significance.

With it all he was an unassuming man; but when
one considers how history has passed him by, modesty
seems a doubtful virtue. Had he been less reticent and
more prolific as a letter writer, posterity long ago
might have had more enlightenment as to his deeds
and have rated him, as he should be rated, an emi-
nently successful officer of the Continental navy.

Similarly, the *Saratoga* has been mistreated. She
has been called variously a brig, a sloop, a ship, and a
sloop-of-war by these same historians and biographers
who have fumbled with her captain's name. Actually
she was ship-rigged, but classified as a sloop-of-war, a
naval designation which bears little relation to rigging.
The only claim to glory advanced for her to date seems
to be that she was the first of a half dozen American
naval vessels bearing her name. Her most famous descendants were the flagship of Thomas Macdonough's
little fleet on Lake Champlain in 1814, and the famous
"Sara" of World War II—that aircraft carrier which
survived Jap bomb and torpedo to perish in an atomic

test at Eniwetok. And now the name is to be perpetu-
ated in a 60,000 ton supercarrier—a far cry, indeed,
from John Young's little *Saratoga* of about 150 tons
burden.

WILLIAM BELL CLARK

Brevard, North Carolina.

Acknowledgments

THAT I have been able to rescue John Young and the sloop-of-war *Saratoga* from oblivion is due in no small measure to the willing co-operation of a number of people to whom I wish to extend my deepest gratitude. They include Marion V. Brewington of Cambridge, Maryland, who read the original draft of this manuscript and contributed many helpful suggestions; Miss Dorothy C. Barck, librarian of the New York Historical Society, whose knowledge of the Rodney Papers in the Public Records Office, London, afforded many helpful clues in ferreting out a true picture of one of John Young's most sensational cruises; William S. Mason, formerly of Evanston, Illinois, who most generously granted me liberal access to his magnificent Franklin collection now housed at Yale University; and all the following, who went to great trouble to supply a persistent and, sometimes, annoying author with every book, pamphlet, or manuscript in which he thought might be found reference to John Young: Commodore Dudley W. Knox, U.S.N. (ret.), formerly in charge of the Naval Records and Library, Navy Department, Washington; J. Harcourt Givens and Miss Catharine H. Miller, of the Manuscript Division of the Historical Society of Pennsylvania, Philadelphia; Mrs. Gertrude D. Hess, assistant librarian of the American Philosophical Society, Philadelphia; Arthur S. Maynard, executive secretary of the New York Genealogical and Biographical Society; Fred E. Manning, retired, former chief of the consolidated files of the General Accounting Office, Washington; and Joseph C. Wolf, in charge of the Genealogical Department of the Newberry Library, Chicago.

Table of Contents

Preface		*v*
I	The Captain Gets a Command	1
II	The Years Before	10
III	The New Sloop-of-War	23
IV	Gentlemen All!	33
V	The Strategy of Francis Lewis	47
VI	The First Cruise	61
VII	The Sea-Fighter	71
VIII	Prizes and Prisoners	89
IX	£500,000 Security!	104
X	The Sea-Fighter Sails South	118
XI	The Last Cruise	131
XII	The Curtain Falls	141
Appendices		151
Notes		159
Bibliography		181
Index		191

CHAPTER I

The Captain Gets a Command

THREE events of naval significance took place in Philadelphia in the late fall of 1779.

The Marine Committee of Congress, which had struggled for four years, with indifferent success, to maintain an effective navy, was succeeded by a Board of Admiralty, for which there were high hopes.[1]

The keel was laid in the Continental shipyard at Southwark for a sloop-of-war, which had been authorized in 1776, but, because of the precarious state of the Treasury, had remained on the drawing board ever since.[2]

And the Navy Board of the Middle District, after a long-delayed inquiry, exonerated Captain John Young of all blame in the loss of the Continental brig *Independence* on Ocracoke Bar in North Carolina in the spring of 1778.[3]

The import of the first two items loomed large in the mind of the captain, who had just been cleared. The chairman of the new Board of Admiralty was Francis Lewis of New York who had been Young's friend and sponsor since long before the outbreak of the Revolution.[4] With the shadow which had beclouded his future for eighteen months finally removed, John Young felt himself entitled to active service and hoped he could

count upon Lewis' sympathetic approval of that am-
bition. In weighing his chances, Young considered the
various vessels of the much diminished navy and concluded that his best opportunity lay right at home
where the sloop-of-war was building under the able
direction of Joshua Humphreys, who had designed
the thirteen frigates authorized by Congress in 1775.[5]

Securing that vessel, or any vessel in fact, now
would depend upon how many of the twenty-two captains outranking him on the famous seniority list of
October 10, 1776, were awaiting assignment. He had
learned that "it is the intention of Congress not to
make any new Officers in the Navy until those already
commissioned are put into employment." Accordingly,
in August the Marine Committee had begun compil-
ing a list of all officers then in active or private service,
or who had resigned or been dismissed.[6]

Young named over "the Captains to the Southward"—those outside New England—and felt encouraged. Originally there had been twelve his senior
from the Southern area. Two of them were dead:
Lambert Wickes, lost in the *Reprisal,* on October 1,
1777, and Nicholas Biddle, killed on board the *Randolph,* on March 7, 1778. Five were in command of
Continental vessels: James Nicholson, just appointed
to the frigate *Trumbull;* Thomas Read, assigned to
the frigate *Bourbon,* then being built in Connecticut; John Barry, still more recently sent to the seventy-four gun ship on the ways in New Hampshire;
John Paul Jones, last reported as commanding the
Bon Homme Richard on a cruise out of France, and
James Robinson, captain of the small sloop *Fly.* Three
were in private employ: Charles Alexander, James

Josiah, and Isaiah Robinson. One, William Hallock, was no longer in the service, and the whereabouts of another, John Hodge, was not known.[7]

The "Captains to the Northward"—the New Englanders—did not worry him. They were pretty much in the ill graces of Congress for their persistent tactics in sending most of their prizes into Boston, "which thereby Abounds with West India produce, whilst this, port [Philadelphia] tho in the vicinity of Head Quarters are so destitute of those Articles necessary for the Army, that the commissioners are obliged to purchase here at double the Boston prices."[8] Of the ten New Englanders who had outranked him only one, Abraham Whipple, was in active Continental service as commander of the frigate *Providence.* Five of them—Hector McNeill, Thomas Thompson, Dudley Saltonstall, John Burroughs Hopkins, and Joseph Olney—either had been broken by court martial or were under suspension; another, John Manley, was a prisoner of war.[9] Only three awaited employment—Elisha Hinman, Hoysteed Hacker, and Thomas Grennell. But Hinman was out of favor in Philadelphia;[10] Hacker recently had lost the sloop *Providence* in the ill-fated Penobscot expedition,[11] and Grennell seems to have gone into voluntary retirement.[12]

So Young, with mingled hopes and doubts, haunted the Southwark shipyard—it was not far from his home in Laurel street—watching and wishing as the new sloop-of-war began to take shape upon the stocks. Her construction had been authorized in a resolution passed by Congress on November 20, 1776,[13] but not a step had been taken toward carrying out the resolution until July 1, 1779. On that date, the Navy Board had

issued instructions for the building of a "Brigantine of
67 feet Keel to Carry 16 Six pounder Cannon, to be
Constructed in Such manner as Mr Humphreys the
Master Builder May think proper."[14]

Even then no progress had been made for some
months because money as usual had been scarce. Prospects now were brighter, for on December 13, the
Board of Treasury had issued a warrant on the man-
agers of the United States lottery for $50,000 in favor
of the Board of Admiralty for the use of the Navy
Board of the Middle District. Humphreys, departing
from the original instructions, was building a ship of
sixty-eight foot keel instead of a brigantine of sixty-
seven feet. She had a beam of twenty-five feet, four
inches, and a twelve-foot depth in hold. Other details
the master-builder had set down in his neat hand:
"Center of the foremast 13 feet abaft the after part of
the Spirketing[,] center of main mast abaft center of
foremast 35 feet & center of mizen mast 24' 7" abaft
center of main mast." He intended to mast her with
main, top, and topgallant masts, which would extend
better than one hundred feet above the deck. Her
foremast, with top and topgallant masts would be six
feet shorter, and her mizzenmast with topmast would
lift about seventy-five feet in the air. Bowsprit, jib
boom and yards, including royals, would be commen-
surate in length with the masts.[15]

By December only the ship's ribs were in place, but
Young could visualize her completed and yearned for
assurance she would be his to command. Such assurance could come only from the new Board of Admiralty, which was as yet without a quorum. In fact,
it was without almost everything save a chairman, two

Congressional members, and a secretary.[16] But December slipped by with no word. The Board of Admiralty now was involved in budget-making. Congress wanted an estimate of the amount of money needed to operate the navy economically for a year. Such an estimate had to be the work of Lewis and the secretary, John Brown, for the two Congressional members were seldom in attendance. Other members-at-large either had not been selected or had, so far, failed to accept appointment. It was January 3, 1780, before the estimate was completed.[17]

During this period of waiting, Young found time heavy on his hands. There were no fellow officers of equal rank in the city for companionship, and there was not a single Continental vessel in port. The last of these to leave had been the frigate *Confederacy,* Captain Seth Harding, which had sailed for France on October 26, 1779, carrying as passengers retiring Ambassador Conrad Alexandre Gérard and his suite, and John Jay, newly appointed American Minister to Spain.[18] In Gérard's place had come the Chevalier César Anne de la Luzerne, whose arrival in Philadelphia in September had been occasion for much éclat—"the sound of bells" and an escort of cavalry "composed of the most important citizens of the town."[19] It was November 17, however, before Luzerne had been formally introduced to Congress.[20] Young had witnessed some of the ceremonials and receptions which the new Ambassador staged in the mansion set aside for his residence "at the western edge of the city, almost opposite that in which the State and the Congress hold their sessions and spend their days in blessing France and cursing England."[21]

Though little information exists regarding John Young's activities during the winter of 1779-80, it appears that he had found a congenial spirit in the person of William Semple, a merchant in Front street, whose influence was apparent thereafter in the captain's commercial transactions. Semple had been "out" with the militia during the Flying Camp of 1776—had commanded a company, in fact[22]—but since then had stuck to his mercantile enterprises. He had begun to look a bit enviously at fellow merchants who were reaping fortunes in privateering, and Young was a good man to advise him on that score. The first record of their friendship is on December 1, 1779,[23] and, as will be seen, this friendship in time proved profitable to both.

Shortly before, Young had made a real estate investment in "10 Lots of Ground in the Northern Liberties." These lots lay on the north side of Brown street and up along the east side of Fourth street. They were part of the estate of Samuel Shoemaker, an attainted traitor and former alderman of Philadelphia. William Coates had acquired them first on June 29, 1779, and had sold them to Young for about £300 on November 1.[24] The Northern Liberties, lying just north of the city proper, was considered the natural direction for its expansion. Since not long afterwards the state assessed the land for taxation at £500, the purchase seemed a good investment.[25]

While Young invested in new property, there was little activity on the northern war fronts. The eighteenth century habit of adjourning operations in cold climates during the winter season militated against any major movements, though prospects for a campaign along the southern coast were good. Four vessels of the navy—the frigates *Providence, Boston,* and *Queen of France,* and the ship *Ranger*—had been dispatched from Boston to reinforce the American forces at Charleston, South Carolina, "the Salvation of that State" in a great measure depending "on these Vessels arriving there before the enemy can send any reinforcements."[26] In reviewing the remaining naval strength, there was little cause for optimism. Disregarding the three vessels on the ways at Portsmouth, Middletown and Philadelphia, the Continental navy in northern waters consisted of just two vessels of force. One was the frigate *Trumbull,* outfitting at New London, Connecticut, under the command of James Nicholson.[27] The other was Samuel Nicholson's frigate *Deane,* which lay at Boston unable to sail because she lacked "a full supply of Bread."[28]

It was altogether a disheartening picture, not only to John Young, but to Francis Lewis, who, undoubtedly, subscribed heartily to what Elbridge Gerry, member of Congress from Massachusetts, was writing to one of his constituents at that time. "The State of our Finances," opined Gerry, would check the present growth of the navy, "but I doubt not that it will soon flourish and that Time will suggest Improvements in the Arrangements and Regulations of the Boards that are appointed to cherish and conduct it."[29] The state of the finances was already slowing up construction upon the new sloop-of-war at Philadelphia, and the Board of Admiralty reported to Congress on January 7 that unless one hundred thousand dollars was forthcoming for the Navy Board of the Middle District, the business of that body would be "intirely at a Stand."[30] To make the navy "flourish" Lewis had then turned from budget-making and emergency appropriations to completing the return of officers begun by the Marine Committee months before. He presented his recommendations to Congress on January 24, and the next day that body concurred in and adopted his resolution "That the pay of all Officers of the Navy not in actual Service cease from this day; that such Officers retain their rank, depositing their Commissions in the respective Navy Boards untill they shall be called into actual Service."[31]

In another two weeks, Lewis was to realize that all the legislation in the world could not bring about flourishing conditions as fast as the hand of Providence could wreck them. Just when he had begun to believe he was making progress, a letter was delivered to him from William Bingham, the Continental agent in Martinique, announcing the arrival at St. Pierre on December 19, 1779, of the frigate *Confederacy* with its rudder split and minus all its masts, its bowsprit, and its spars.[32] Later more details came from John Jay, whose ministerial mission to Spain had been delayed by the accident to the frigate. The ship had been going "nine knots an hour in a brisk breeze and rough sea, but by no means hard weather, . . ." Jay reported; when, off the Newfoundland banks on November 7, "her bowsprit and all her masts gave way in less than three minutes." A gale came on during the ensuing night, and "the next morning the shank of the rudder was found to be so much wrenched and split, that the Captain told me he thought it a greater misfortune than the loss of the masts."[33] Faced with the necessity of ordering new masts to be sent out from New England to Martinique, it is not surprising to find the Board of Admiralty writing to the Navy Board of the Eastern Department at Boston that "to satisfy your repeated calls for money is really at this time not in their power." As an added note of warning, the letter concluded, "without the strictest Œconomy in future the Credit of these United States cannot be supported."[34]

To John Young, who was well aware of the unhappy state of the navy, a summons came in late February to attend the Navy Board of the Middle District. Young was familiar with the Congressional mandate regarding officers not in actual service. Was he to be recalled to duty, or would he be asked to surrender his commission? Ready for either eventuality, he presented himself before the same three men who had conducted the inquiry into the loss of the *Independence*: John Wharton, Humphreys' partner in the Southwark shipyard; James Read, who in the earlier years of the war had been the navy's paymaster; and William Winder, Jr. One of the three board members —we know not which one—broke the news.

By direction of the Board of Admiralty, it gave them great pleasure to inform him that he was now formally assigned to the command of the new sloop-of-war being built at Philadelphia.[35]

CHAPTER II

The Years Before

C APTAIN of a ship still on the ways—a ship
without a name and without a crew!
With that prospect John Young returned to the
Continental service. Much had happened before that
time; much which has to be understood before the captain's intense desire to sail again in a Continental fighting vessel can be appreciated.

Who was John Young? Francis Lewis could have
satisfied such an inquiry that fall a lot easier than it
can be done now. That hardy, sixty-six year old
Welshman, who had sailed the seas himself in building
his own commercial house, knew the shipmasters of
New York and had employed many of them.[1] Of them
all, John Young was his favorite from the day in 1768,
when he had come across the youngster as a mate in
the West India trade, sailing under James Scott, master of the brig *Tobago* to the Grenades.[2]

Exploration today into Young's ancestry and an-
tecedents presents a formidable, if not baffling task for
the most ardent genealogist. His wife, Joanna Mann
Young, whom he married in the old Dutch Reformed
Church, in New York City on February 7, 1771,[3] survived him but left few details of her husband's life.
Appealing years afterwards to Congress for a widow's

half-pay, she set forth simply that her husband, "at an early period of the late glorious Revolution entered on board the Continental Sloop of War the Independence."[4] In drawing up his will in 1780, Young laid no greater claim to fame than to designate himself as "of the City of Philadelphia, Mariner."[5] That he identified himself as a Philadelphian was wartime necessity. He was a native of New York and of Dutch descent, but that city had been in the enemy's possession for four years.

John Young was bred to the sea and quite early gave strong indications of superiority in his profession. As a youth he learned to read, write, and cipher. It is apparent from his letters that no schoolmaster labored greatly to teach him orthography, but unlike most seafaring men of his day, he did not spell euphoniously.[6] By contemporaries he was considered impetuous, venturesome, and courageous—"full of ardor," as one put it. That he was highly intelligent, resourceful, companionable, and yet a disciplinarian, events will show. We have no notion of his physical appearance. The inventory of his estate listed eleven pictures; whether or not one was a portrait of him will never be known, for no likeness of him has been preserved.[7]

His qualifications for a Continental commission were as good as, if not better than, many a master in the merchant marine who had been honored by Congress with a command. He sailed in the brig *Tobago* from 1768 until 1772,[8] when the more attractive berth as first mate of the ship *America,* William Hervey, master, came along.[9] Three transatlantic voyages— two to Hull and one to Bristol—widened his horizon and gave him the needed experience to sail his own

ship. He said farewell to Captain Hervey in the fall
of 1773—just about the time first repercussions of the
tea act aroused the colonies—and received his master's
certificate in October. His command was the ninety-
ton brig *Elizabeth,* just launched, of which Francis
Lewis was part owner.[10] Young promptly signified
his elevation to master by joining the Marine Society
of the City of New York, the exclusive organization
of shipmasters formed to care for the widows or wives
and children of deceased or indigent members.[11]

The widening breach between mother country and
colonies manifested itself to him more clearly upon
every voyage of the *Elizabeth.* Before she sailed on
her maiden trip, he and his wife had witnessed the
burning in effigy of a Manhattan merchant, then so-
journing in London, who urged enforcement of the
hated tea tax.[12] At Charleston, South Carolina, he
watched the confiscation of the first tea cargo to arrive
there.[13] Young was at Gosport, in old England, when
news of Boston's Tea Party arrived.[14] He returned to
New York as delegates to the first Continental Congress set off for Philadelphia to the cheers of the
citizens.[15] Finally, in 1775, during a rapid voyage to
London, before the Continental Association closed off
all intercourse, he saw the stunned reaction of the British when they learned that the rebels had dared to re-
sort to arms.[16]

Upon the return voyage Young made his decision.
There could be no more employment for the *Elizabeth.*
Both the Continental Association and the British navy
had seen to that. He knew the might and power of the
mother country. He had seen her grand fleet at Spit-
head. He had sensed the determination of King and

Ministry to crush the revolt. He had no illusions as to colonial strength, even with all thirteen provinces united; yet, on that western passage of the *Elizabeth,* another rebel was born.

Francis Lewis gave him his first employment in the American cause—a commission to bring powder and arms from France. He sailed in a small sloop in the winter of 1775-76 for L'Orient and returned the following May to Egg Harbor, New Jersey, with a cargo of thirteen tons of gunpowder, twenty-five tons of saltpeter, and sixty stand of arms.[17] A skipper responsible for arrival of a supply of those indispensables large enough to keep a Continental wagon master busy for two weeks hauling them from Egg Harbor could advance considerable claim for recognition.[18] The influence of Francis Lewis and of both Marine and Secret Committees of Congress in addition to this formed a logical sequence, which resulted in a commission as a captain in the Continental navy on July 23, 1776.[19]

His first command, a small sloop converted to war purposes, had been named the *Independence*—a word fresh, inspiring, and indicative of an accomplished legislative fact. That it had been bestowed upon one of the smallest craft on the Continental register might have been incongruous had it not been almost symbolic of the disparity in strength between the infant thirteen United States of North America and Great Britain.[20]

The *Independence* had the reputation of a fast sailer, an armament of ten iron 4-pounder carriage guns, and a crew of about thirty.[21] Young took her to sea in October, 1776, bound for Martinique with a cargo of tobacco and bar iron to be exchanged for "all the good Arms & Gunlocks, Powder, Gun Flints, Salt petre Sulphur—Sail Cloth Blankets, or other woolin goods," that could be crammed into her hold.[22]

Southward bound he took his first prize and sent her into Philadelphia.[23] At Martinique he fell ill and, knowing the need of his cargo at home, he dispatched the *Independence* under her first lieutenant. It was a hard decision for a man ambitious for success, but it was a happy one, resulting in a signal service to George Washington. The *Independence* entered the Delaware late in December, at a time when the British were threatening Philadelphia. Robert Morris, who had stayed behind in the panicky city when Congress decamped to Baltimore, rushed sixteen bales of blankets from the sloop's cargo to army headquarters. They arrived on Christmas Day of 1776. That night, Washington embarked his army in boats and crossed the Delaware to fight the battle of Trenton.[24]

Young recovered and returned to Philadelphia early in 1777; he resumed command of the *Independence* in time to be sent upon another voyage to Martinique in March.[25] This time he remained well, but, homeward bound, he was driven into Sinepuxent Bay, Maryland, when a British squadron blocked the Delaware capes. He carried as cargo two thousand stand of arms and five hundred tents,[26] and, just before slipping into Sinepuxent, he made prize of a small schooner.[27]

After the arms and tents had been carted off to Philadelphia, Young was ordered to stand by for important dispatches for France. They reached him early in July, but lack of supplies held him in port until almost mid-August. The long delay, however, enabled him to be of service again to Washington. Howe's British fleet—warships and transports to the number of 228—passed down the coast in plain view of the little sloop in Sinepuxent Bay. Young's letter, reporting the whereabouts of the enemy, reached the American army in time to halt its northward march and focus anew the attention of the Commander in Chief on the peril to Philadelphia.[28]

The voyage to France was uneventful, save for the capture of two British merchant vessels, one of which was later retaken.[29] The *Independence* entered the Loire on September 24, after a passage of forty-five days.[30] Young's orders were to deliver his packet in person to the American Commissioners at Paris and return to the *Independence* to await their dispatches. He performed the journey expeditiously, but the return dispatches were slow in arriving,[31] so he utilized the time in having the *Independence* converted into a brig.[32] While he idled in the Loire, a small sloop arrived from Boston with the momentous news of Burgoyne's surrender at Saratoga, and the *Independence*'s little guns blazed joyously at the tidings. A week later John Paul Jones sailed up the Loire in the Continental ship *Ranger*.[33] They had met before; in fact, Jones had spent much time with the Youngs in Philadelphia in the summer of 1776 and had fallen in love with one of Mistress Young's close friends.[34]

British cruisers in the Bay of Biscay bottled a number of American merchant ships, including the *Independence,* in the Loire; considered too lightly armed to cope with the enemy war vessels, she was held in port, even though her dispatches had arrived.[35] But the news of Saratoga already had brought the French close to an alliance with the United States, and the first fruits of this closer relationship was the promise of a convoy off the French coast by the squadron of La Motte Picquet, then lying in Quiberon Bay.[36]

It was the privilege of John Young in February, 1778, therefore, to share with John Paul Jones in receiving from this French squadron the first salute to the Stars and Stripes. Jones sailed under the admiral's stern at six o'clock in the evening of February 14— about sunset of a gray day—and heralded his arrival with thirteen guns at minute intervals. La Motte Picquet replied with nine. Then, to be sure the French admiral had not accorded him unintentional recognition in the dim light, Jones boarded the *Independence* next day as Young sailed her through the fleet, firing his own 4-pounders thirteen times and receiving a similar return of nine guns.[37]

This high-point of John Young's career as a Continental captain was to be followed by disaster. Young would have liked to continue with Jones, but the latter felt he had no authority to detain the brig in European waters. So, the *Independence* sailed forth with La Motte Picquet's convoying ships on February 25,[38] leaving the convoy early in March off the Azores. Upon advice previously given by Jones, Young then set his course for Ocracoke Inlet on the North Carolina coast.[39] On April 15, the brig was wrecked on Ocracoke Bar.[40] We have no details on why it happened, though a letter written a few months later by John Bondfield, Continental agent at Bordeaux may provide a clue. "It is distressing," he wrote, "to hear the accounts given of Loss's on the coast by the negligence and wilful misconduct of the Pilot's situated on the Pass's on the Carolina Coast we have received few [letters] from them quarters without accompanying [pro]tests of ships Masters against the Inhabitants who in lieu of succouring have frequently misled or refused assistance."[41]

Irrespective of how it happened, Young saved a quantity of the cargo, virtually all stores, the 4-pounders, and even the ship's bell.[42] He had to entrust his dispatches to a passenger, who delivered them to Congress at York, Pennsylvania, and who commented later that "poor Young had the Misfortune to loss the Brig on Ocracok Bar."[43]

It was a great misfortune, and the news of it arrived at a most inappropriate time. Within the previous fortnight, Congress had heard of nothing but American naval disasters. James Nicholson, senior captain in the navy, had run the frigate *Virginia* onto a shoal in Chesapeake Bay, lost his rudder, and apparently his presence of mind as well, and had deserted her in the face of the enemy.[44] Nicholas Biddle had gone to heroic death when the frigate *Randolph* had blown up during an engagement in the West Indies.[45] The ship *Alfred* had been captured when deserted by her consort, the *Raleigh,* upon returning from a voyage to France.[46] The ship *Columbus,* trying to slip past a British blockade in Narragansett Bay, had been chased ashore and burned on Point Judith.[47] Then had come word of the loss of the *Independence* as a culminating blow. "A little Bynging would be of infinite service," wrote William Ellery, Congressional delegate from Rhode Island. Apparently Ellery felt that the execution of the unfortunate Admiral John Byng in 1757 should be a model for American procedure.[48]

John Young was prepared for the curt order the Marine Committee sent him on June 18, directing him to "repair to Baltimore where we have ordered the Navy Board to hold a Court of Inquiry into the Cause of the loss of the late Continental Brigantine under your Command, and if it shall appear that the same was Occasioned by your negligence or mal Conduct or that of any of the Commissioned officers, that then a Court Martial be held for the trial of the Officer offending agreeable to a Resolution of Congress of the 6th of May last."[49]

No court of inquiry was held then, however, because the Navy Board was itself caught in the confusion of returning to Philadelphia after the British evacuation. The Navy Board, the Marine Committee, Congress, and nearly everybody else seemed to converge on the nation's capital, and the captain joined the crowd.[50] There he and his wife, reunited after a separation of more than a year, set up housekeeping while awaiting the summons to appear before the court of inquiry. They purchased a substantial brick residence in Southwark, choosing a location just below the southern boundary of the city, and only a short distance from the Delaware. According to the street nomenclature of the times, their house stood on the west side of Laurel street below Cedar—No. 818, according to an old Philadelphia City Directory.[51] The neighborhood still exists, although Laurel has become South American and Cedar is now South street. Foreign tongues assail the ear in South American street today. No longer is it the desirable location that the Youngs had found it in 1778. Altogether pleasing to them had been their choice then, and evidence that it was a home of some pretension is found in the fact that the state of Pennsylvania assessed a property valuation of £1,200 upon it.[52]

Had the Navy Board of the Middle District given Young's case attention that summer of 1778, matters most likely would have gone badly for him. Fortunately their attention was focused elsewhere—on supplying the French fleet which had just brought M. Gérard, the first French Ambassador to the United States, and on equipping Continental vessels to co-operate with that fleet in naval operations which, although ambitious, never materialized.[53] With no action upon his case likely for some time, Young accepted from Robert Morris the command of a little letter-of-marque schooner called the *Buckskin*.[54] In her, between November 6 and February 10, 1779, he made a voyage to Cuba, notable only because he bought his wife a little Negro boy, about nine years of age.[55] She named the small slave Favorite, which no doubt aptly described the position he soon won in the household as his mistress's pet.[56]

Meanwhile, Mistress Young had been equipping the new home on Laurel street. An inventory of the furnishings exists and from the items enumerated we can largely picture the various rooms. The house was L-shaped and boasted three rooms on the first floor— one behind the other—and four on the second floor.

The living room, which ran across the front of the house, or bottom of the L, contained a broad fireplace, from which protruded a pair of black andirons and beside which stood tongs and shovel. Upon the mantel-piece were a pair of brass candlesticks and a candle snuffer; additional light was supplied by candles in polished brass sconces flanking the fireplace, and around the hearth was a high brass fender. For ex-tremely cold weather, a copper ship's stove stood in one corner. Against the walls reposed three dainty card tables upon which Mistress Young probably kept several glass decanters of choice Madeira wine and some wine glasses. She owned nine such decanters—five quart size and four pint size. An oblong Pembroke table—the inventory called it a "pinebroke table"—with edgings of marquetry stood in the center of the room. Several mahogany chairs and four Windsor chairs completed the major furnishings. Over the fire-place was a mirror, and a half-dozen pictures hung on the walls. Checked curtains draped the three win-dows in the front of the room and the one which opened on the areaway in the rear.

Gracing the dining room was another fireplace, upon whose mantelpiece rested also a pair of brass candlesticks. If Mistress Young displayed all her china upon the plate rail, it must have been filled with ten china plates, three dozen queen's ware plates and eleven queen's ware dishes of various sizes. Upon a little tea table against one wall reposed some of her two dozen china cups and saucers and perhaps her china teapot and sugar bowl. Most likely a built-in cabinet held the remainder as well as three queen's ware tureens, a china bowl, some thirty ounces of silver plate, a "crewet and salts," and a dozen or more wine glasses. In the drawers below were two dozen each of knives and forks and three dozen horn spoons.

A large dining-room table and a half-dozen mahogany chairs completed the furnishings. Light came through three small windows along the areaway, each covered with checked curtains.

In the kitchen were two kitchen tables and five chairs; a fireplace equipped with iron pots and hooks as well as a jack, spit, and skewers; two Dutch ovens, three copper sauce pans, three pairs of smoothing irons, three buckets, six tea cannisters, three copper kettles, and two small brass kettles. And in the basement were two washing tubs, a wood axe, and a hammer.

All four bedrooms were furnished, three with bedsteads, and one with a cot and a ship's hammock. In their own bedroom—probably the one in the front of the house—was a fireplace with brass candlesticks and a snuffer on the mantel. Mistress Young had made it most attractive with chintz curtains for the three windows and a chintz bedspread to match. Several small rugs were on the floor, and there were both dressing and toilet tables. That they and their guests slept well is attested by the fact that the inventory specified "3 Feather Beds Bolsters & pillows." There were counterpanes for guest-room beds, one of which was of "Callicoe." The linens—thirteen pair of sheets, thirteen pair of pillow cases and six blankets—a picture or two, a chair or two, and a mirror for each room completed the second floor inventory.[57]

Young had but a brief space to enjoy the comforts of the Laurel street home. He learned that no court of inquiry was yet in contemplation, so he accepted another letter of marque and sailed for Hispaniola. His vessel was the brig *Impertinent,* of "ten Dubel fortified four Pounders," and a crew of thirty men, sailing under John Barry, commodore by courtesy of rank, in a fleet of five armed vessels for joint protection.[58] Just off the Delaware, Young espied a distant sail, and pursued and took her before his consorts came up. She was His Majesty's sloop-of-war *Harlem,* of fourteen 4-pounders, and she surrendered without firing a gun.[59] Later he landed the prisoners at his old haunt, Sinepuxent Bay, and engaged in a violent altercation with a militia colonel who was loath to accept them from him.[60]

Without further adventure, the little fleet arrived at Port-au-Prince. Upon the return another prize was taken, and subsequently lost again to the enemy. On October 5, 1779, Young sailed the *Impertinent* up the Delaware to Philadelphia and learned from his wife that the Navy Board was ready at last to proceed with the court of inquiry. The subsequent exoneration set the stage for the appointment to the new sloop-of-war building in Southwark.[61]

CHAPTER III

The New Sloop-of-War

MUCH had happened since John Young's debut as a captain in 1776, yet, as he watched his nameless sloop-of-war nearing completion under the supervision of "Mr Humphreys the Master Builder," he realized he was actually back where he had started. Regardless of his exoneration by the court of inquiry, of his good previous record, of his success while sailing under a letter of marque, and of the influential post of his patron, Francis Lewis, on the Board of Admiralty, Young knew his reputation had to be made anew.

The loss of the *Independence* on Ocracoke Bar, although through no fault of his, was not forgotten. In early April, the second anniversary of the disaster, Lewis showed him a letter from the firm of Hewes, Smith & Allen. Vandals had looted the Continental storehouse at Edenton, North Carolina, and sails salvaged from the wreck of the *Independence* were among the stolen property.[1]

Further reminder of the ill-fated brigantine came a little later, when the Board of Admiralty confided to him the name selected for his new command. It conjured up that November day of 1777, when he first heard of Burgoyne's surrender and the *Independence,* anchored in the Loire, had been wreathed in smoke as

her 4-pounders thundered a salute to that great victory. The new sloop-of-war was to be called the *Saratoga.*[2]

With little noise and no acclaim, the *Saratoga* was
launched into the Delaware from the Continental shipyard on Monday, April 10.[3] Present at the ceremony
were Young, the three members of the Navy Board,
Francis Lewis, James Forbes and William Ellery of
the Board of Admiralty, and, of course, the master
builder, Humphreys.[4] Compliments rained upon
Humphreys on the way in which she took the water.
She had trim lines, this Philadelphia-built ship, and
Lewis in particular was vastly enthusiastic about her.
Many a vessel had been constructed in the shipyards
of the Delaware before but never a ship specifically
designed as a sloop-of-war.

The *Saratoga* was afloat, but, in getting her off the
ways, the last penny of the Navy Board's building
appropriation had been used up. How to get her out-
fitted? Lewis wasted no time. Within twenty-four
hours, he was drafting a report to Congress, along
with a definite recommendation. "The Board of Admiralty beg leave to represent to Congress," he wrote,
"that the Continental Ship Saratoga has been lately
launched at this place, and may be speedily fitted for
sea if the Board had money for that purpose. As the
Saratoga in all probability, will be a very fast sailing
vessel and considerable advantages may arise to the
public from her being speedily fitted out the Board
would therefore recommend . . . that the balance of
money in the hands of the Board of Admiralty, arising
from the sale of wines sold under their direction be applied in fitting with despatch the Ship Saratoga."[5]

Congress passed the resolution on April 12,[6] and
the outfitting got under way "with the utmost expedition." Humphreys had designed her to carry sixteen
6-pounders, but Young now suggested 9-pounders,
and the builder agreed she could bear that weight of
metal. There is some confusion in contemporary accounts as to just what the final armament was, but,
upon the most reliable authority, it would seem that
she showed eighteen double fortified iron carriage guns
—sixteen 9-pounders and two 4-pounders.[7]

For work upon her, the carpenters were paid forty-
six dollars a day—a stupendous wage, at first glance
—but it was in Continental currency. In April, 1780,
it took about thirty-eight Continental dollars to equal
a dollar in specie; and the Board of Admiralty, in-
censed over the extravagance displayed at Middletown, Connecticut, in the building of the frigate
Bourbon, held up the *Saratoga* as a model of economy.
The Board, while admitting it "did not expect the people of Connecticut would escape the general conta-
gion," deplored the exorbitant wages paid there, particularly "when it is considered that the Carpenters
there have their rations found them and the expense of
subsisting a family there is not half so great as it is
here."[8] Behind the plaint lay fears that the slipping
value of the Continental dollar was likely to defeat at
the outset the Board of Admiralty's first effort in
naval strategy.

A scheme to gather a sizable fleet at Philadelphia
had been hatching in Francis Lewis' mind for some
weeks. He had pointed out, on March 28, in a letter to
Benjamin Franklin, in Paris, that the "detachment of
four ships to gaurd the harbour of Charles Town has

subjected our Coasts to the depredations of the enemys armed Vessels from New York who of late have frequently appeared in our bays." His letter to the American Minister Plenipotentiary had, in fact, specifically requested the return of the frigate *Alliance* from European waters, and had named Philadelphia as her destination.[9] Early in April, the Board of Admiralty accordingly proposed to assemble a squadron of sufficient size to sweep the Delaware and southern New Jersey coasts free from an infestation of "Armed Vessels from New York who have made many valuable Captures."[10]

In his calculations the Chairman of the Board figured the end of June as the earliest possible time for the rendezvous and omitted any thought of the vessels in South Carolina waters. To even the most sanguine, it was apparent in April that the ships at Charleston were bottled up.[11] Discounting them, however, Lewis counted upon the *Trumbull,* from New London; the *Deane,* from Boston; the *Confederacy,* from Martinique; the *Alliance,* from France; and possibly the *Bourbon,* from Middletown. These, plus the *Saratoga,* would comprise a formidable squadron. The *Trumbull* was "compleatly rigged, wooded & Watered with 120 men on board officers included, and . . . she only waited for some additional provisions & Cannon which . . . will be on board in three weeks." So, on April 17, instructions were sent off by post to James Nicholson at New London:

"As the Continental Ship Saratoga Captain John Young is now launched and fitting . . . the Board intend that Ship to Cruize in concert with the Trumbull, therefore you are hereby directed to make a short

Cruize in such latitudes as you think will be most likely to annoy the enemy, and afterward come into Delaware towards the latter end of the Month of June, in Order to join the Saratoga and any other of the Continental ships which may be here at that time." [12]

First to reach the Delaware, despite numerous rumors that she was headed for Boston, was the *Confederacy*. She proved a keen disappointment. Makeshift and inferior masts had been stepped into place at Martinique, and one of these had been sprung on the homeward voyage. To climax the ill luck, she had lost her best bow anchor on April 26, when a gale had driven her from her moorings under Cape Henlopen while she awaited a pilot to bring her up the bay.[13] When she reached Chester three days later, Lewis almost threw up his hands in despair. John Young, viewing her at the same time, could scarcely believe she was the same trim frigate he had seen in the Delaware seven months earlier. Putting her into shape again would take far longer and cost a great deal more than expected for various cables and anchors were not procurable this side of Boston.[14]

Undaunted by the crippled condition of the *Confederacy,* Francis Lewis continued to display rare optimism over the Board of Admiralty scheme for squadron operations. News that the *Deane* had returned to Boston from a short but successful cruise fired him with renewed zeal. Congratulating Samuel Nicholson upon his good fortune, the Board wrote him on May 12 that the Navy Board of the Eastern Department had been directed to fit out the *Deane* as rapidly as possible and to have her in Delaware Bay by the end

of June. The letter enumerated the various vessels expected at the rendezvous and remarked that it relied
upon him to arrive in time.[15]

A week later, the other Nicholson was causing con-
cern. Captain James Nicholson had written from New
London on May 3 that he was ready for sea but that
he was going on a cruise with the privateer *General
Mifflin*. Off to him went a terse command on May 22:
"We now repeat our former Order vizt. that you make
a short Cruize so as to return to the Delaware" by the
end of June.[16] The order reached New London too
late. On May 12, in blithe disregard of instructions,
"The Trumbull frigate, Captain Nicholson, of 32
guns, 24 of which are 12 pounders & the Mifflin privateer of 20 guns, sailed from New London . . . to cruise
off Sandy Hook, in hopes of falling in with his Majesty's ships the Galatea and Delight."[17]

While Lewis, with commendable pertinacity, pushed
his plans for a squadron cruise, the Chevalier de la
Luzerne announced to Congress on May 16 that a
long-hoped-for event was about to be realized—a
French army under the Count de Rochambeau, and
a French squadron, under the Chevalier de Ternay,
were upon the high seas, bound for America, to help
"put an end by effectual measures to the calamities of
the present war." Just where along the coast this
French expeditionary force might put in appearance,
the Ambassador could not say, but he wanted secrecy
and preparation by Congress so that the two nations,
closely united, could bring "their combined enterprises
to a successful issue."[18]

The inevitable committee was appointed, and still
more inevitable conferences followed; on May 24, the

report upon co-operation with the French allies was submitted. It dealt pretty largely with naval matters. Because "every means should be used to add to the strength of the fleet of our Ally on their arrival, particularly by completing the Ship America," the committee offered resolutions: the Board of Admiralty should fit all ships of war for sea with the utmost expedition; the states wherein vessels of war were being built or fitted out should aid the Board in this important task; Congress would reimburse the states for every outlay, and, finally, "the Board of Admiralty [should] be empowered, if they shall think it advisable to dispose of the Saratoga, to apply the proceeds thereof to complete the America, or any of the frigates, which may by that means be shortly fitted for sea.[19]

From Wednesday until Saturday, May 27, Congress took no action but on the latter day decided that "so much of the report as relates to the disposal of the Saratoga be referred to the Board of Admiralty."[20] News of the proposal leaked out, and John Young heard about it with a sinking heart. Was the chance to rehabilitate his reputation to be taken from him? Was the *Saratoga,* upon whose outfitting he was lavishing such care, to be sold so that the seventy-four gun ship-of-the-line at Portsmouth, or the frigate at Middletown could be completed or the damaged *Confederacy* repaired?

The Captain set off to see Francis Lewis. Lewis admitted that there was no money available for finishing the *America* and the *Bourbon,* but he set Young's fears at rest. The *Saratoga* would *not* be sold. Since the Board of Admiralty had been forced to wipe the

Providence, the *Boston,* the *Queen of France,* and the *Ranger* off the naval register (for news of the loss of Charleston had just been received), the American navy was reduced enough. Lewis had no intention of relinquishing a vessel for which he had high hopes in such an emergency. Moreover, the Board of Admiralty had appealed to New Hampshire, Massachusetts, and Connecticut on May 30 to supply funds to complete the vessels building and outfit the *Deane*.[21] As to the *Confederacy,* there was some prize wine being sold in New London, and the Continental agent there had been directed to send the "whole Money Arising from said sale" immediately to Philadelphia "under a Safe gaurd if necessary." That should be sufficient to "fit out and Man two Ships of war now in this port"; in other words, both the *Confederacy* and the *Saratoga*.[22]

Lewis was determined that the fleet should rendezvous in the Delaware by the end of June. He said so repeatedly, and he reiterated it once more on June 16, in a letter to the Navy Board of the Eastern Department: "We wish to collect the Trumbull Deane Confederacy and Saratoga, at the Capes by the last of the Month to Cruize in Concert."[23] But he was husbanding his few remaining Continental dollars. No officers, other than Young, were in active service on the *Saratoga,* and none would be until the sloop-of-war was almost ready for sea. Almost all the commissioned personnel had been decided upon but not yet called to the colors. Neither would a crew be signed on until the last minute. The Board of Admiralty's slim funds could not stand the strain of another payroll—it was costing too much to accommodate the hands of the

Confederacy while that vessel was being extensively overhauled and repaired.[24]

Confidence restored, John Young returned to the equipping of his sloop-of-war. Despite financial stringency, he made noticeable progress; from Boston came cheering word that work on the *Deane* was going forward swiftly. By mid-June, Lewis could begin to see his plans taking actual shape. The *Confederacy*'s bottom was "compleately graved" by the night of June 16, and her masts were all ready. But best of all, it looked as if "the Saratoga will fall down to Rheedy [*sic*] Island in ten days."[25]

As the time for the rendezvous neared, however, the Board of Admiralty Chairman began to fume. The *Alliance* was still abroad. The *Bourbon* was still on the ways. The *Deane* had not left Boston. Nothing had been heard from the *Trumbull* already overdue at the Delaware Capes. The *Confederacy*'s new masts were not finished after all. Even the *Saratoga*'s fitting was behind schedule. To cap the climax, on the last day of the month—the very day he had set for the rendezvous—Lewis received two letters from Boston. One came from the Navy Board of the Eastern Department, and the other from James Nicholson. The *Trumbull* had put into that port on June 14, her masts shot away and eight of her men killed and thirty wounded, after a bloody five-hour engagement with a heavily armed British merchant ship.[26] It was small consolation to learn later that the *Trumbull*'s opponent, the ship *Watt*, had suffered far more severely.[27]

The joint cruise off the coast had received a decided setback, but Lewis, still determined, urged James Nicholson to the utmost exertion in refitting, that "your ship may be here in proper Season and in Company with the Deane." He did not even censure the senior captain of the navy for disobedience of orders, probably because of the gallantry displayed in the engagement and "the honor arising therefrom to the flag of the United States."[28]

The persistent Chairman of the Board of Admiralty merely moved his rendezvous date ahead a month or two and turned his attention to manning the *Saratoga* and putting the *Confederacy* into service. Even so, he realized that delay was rendering the joint cruise still more uncertain; already Congress had thought of another use for one of his frigates. By resolution of June 24, the Board of Admiralty had been directed to send a Continental vessel to Cap François to bring back "a very considerable quantity of Merchandize belonging to the United States, as also the materials for completely equipping two Frigates of 36 guns each."[29]

Lewis had known about this equipment in the hands of one Carabasse, the Beaumarchais agent at the Cap, for more than a month. He had, on June 1, written to Carabasse to ship the goods by "every good opportunity," hoping to avoid the necessity of sending a Continental vessel after them and thus spoiling his pet scheme.[30] He had urged the Navy Board of the Eastern Department to send some kind of a conveyance from Boston to Cap François.[31] Now, all he could do was report to Congress that he had no frigate available for the mission and then trust fervently that Carabasse would get his precious stores off to the American continent before a Continental ship could be made ready.

CHAPTER IV

Gentlemen All!

THE public interest, said venerable William Livingston, wartime Governor of New Jersey, in consigning his youngest son to a midshipman's berth in the *Saratoga,* "requires our navy to be officered by the children of respectable families."[1] His was not a new thought, for the Continental navy originally boasted a Biddle, a Hopkins, a Saltonstall, and a Wickes, but he voiced it for the first time. In selecting the commissioned personnel of the new sloop-of-war, therefore, John Young and the Board of Admiralty kept the dictum of New Jersey's chief executive in mind. All through June they had been choosing officers whose presence on board would add prestige to the naval service, but not until the beginning of July were the appointments announced. Seven states were represented, and with a single exception the officers were youthful—a fact carrying with it the implication of enthusiasm, valor, and impetuosity.

The first lieutenant was Joshua Barney.[2] Born July 6, 1759, the son of William Barney, prosperous country gentleman of near Baltimore, Maryland, young Barney was just twenty-one years old when he was called to the *Saratoga.*[3] He had spent five years in the Continental navy—fifteen months of them as a prisoner of war.⁴ Shipping as master's mate in the Continental sloop *Hornet,* in the fall of 1775, he had served in turn as master's mate in the *Wasp,* second lieutenant in the *Sachem,* second lieutenant in the *Andrew Doria,* and second lieutenant in the frigate *Virginia.* His initial experience as a prisoner of war had come in December, 1777, when he was captured in one of the *Andrew Doria's* prizes. In March, 1778, when the *Virginia* was captured, Barney had elected to remain with the frigate on a shoal in Chesapeake Bay rather than join James Nicholson in rowing ashore. Exchanged in the fall of 1778, he had sailed again aboard a letter of marque ship. In March, 1780, he had married Anne, daughter of Gunning Bedford, a prominent Philadelphia alderman.⁵

Before accepting his new appointment, Barney presented a wage problem to the Board of Admiralty. The navy owed him two years' pay, which, as he pointed out, "in the present depreciated state of the currency" was not worth receiving.⁶ What bothered him chiefly was the matter of future emoluments—a question of particular moment to a young benedict who, through carelessness, had just been robbed of every penny he owned.⁷ Under naval regulations, the pay of a lieutenant automatically was lowered when serving in a vessel of less than twenty guns. To Barney, who had been a lieutenant in a frigate of twenty-eight guns, it meant a considerable reduction to go out in a sloop-of-war of only eighteen. He pointed out the injustice to the Board of Admiralty and was told he could receive no satisfaction except through Congressional order. Nothing daunted, he petitioned the latter body to "fix his rank and ascertain the pay he shall receive."[8] Congress asked the Board of Admiralty for its recommendation,[9] and the matter was cleared up finally, for Barney and for any other officer in a like dilemma, when Congress ruled "That any officer who, by virtue of his commission or warrant, hath served, or hereafter shall serve, on board any ship of war of 20 guns and upwards, belonging to the navy of these states, and shall hereafter serve in the same rank on board any other vessel of war of inferior force, such officer shall receive the same pay as he was entitled to when serving in a ship of 20 guns and upwards; any resolution to the contrary notwithstanding."[10]

Young Blaney Allison, commissioned as second lieutenant of the sloop-of-war, was also a beneficiary of this Congressional resolve. Lieutenant Allison, nephew of the late celebrated Dr. Francis Allison, Vice Provost and Professor of Moral Philosophy of the College of Philadelphia and onetime Chaplain of the Continental Congress,[11] like Barney, had seen long service in the Continental navy. As a youngster, he had joined the Pennsylvania navy, being appointed on February 26, 1776, a midshipman on board the ship *Montgomery.* Six months later he was discharged "to go with Captain Read" in the Continental service.[12] Under Thomas Read, he served for a few months as a master's mate in the frigate *Washington,* and on December 20, 1776, was commissioned a lieutenant.[13] He seems to have served as a junior officer in the *Washington* until that frigate was scuttled in the Delaware in November, 1777. Thereafter the record is vague, indicating only that at one time he was a prisoner in New York[14] and apparently had been exchanged shortly before joining the *Saratoga.*[15]

From one of New Jersey's old Dutch families came
the sloop-of-war's lieutenant of marines, Abraham
Van Dyke. He had arrived in Philadelphia in June
with a warm letter of recommendation from Washington, who felt that a captaincy of marines would be
"some compensation for the hardships and losses which
he had experienced on account of his steady adherence
to the cause of his country."[16] To please his Excellency, Francis Lewis drew up a captain's commission
for Van Dyke and sent it to Congress for confirmation. It was returned unsigned.[17] Lewis knew why.
A sloop-of-war of under twenty guns rated only a
lieutenant of marines. But Washington had urged a
captaincy, so back to Congress went Lewis to cham-
pion his man. Figuring it merely a matter of dollars,
he suggested a compromise, namely, "that Mr. Van
Dyck be appointed a captain of marines, to act at
present and receive pay as lieutenant of marines on
board the Saratoga." He fortified his recommendation
with some observations. General Washington had
urged the higher rank. He had the General's letter
to prove it. And anyhow, there were but two captains
and two lieutenants of marines out of employment,
"and where they are or in what business engaged is
altogether uncertain."[18]

Congress conferred, debated, and voted on the matter. New Hampshire and North Carolina said "ay"
on the captaincy recommendation. New Jersey was
divided. The other nine states present voted "no." So,
as the clerk recorded it, "it passed in the negative."
A much chastened Lewis returned on July 24 and
urged that Van Dyke be commissioned a lieutenant.
Congress, to be gracious, not only approved the ap-

pointment, but authorized that the commission be dated July 7, "from which time he has acted in that capacity, by order of the Board of Admiralty, on board the Saratoga, sloop of war." [19]

Abraham Van Dyke was well along in years—the exception to the youthful commissioned personnel. He was born in 1719, the son of Jan Van Dyke and Anna Verkerk Van Dyke, a stalwart Dutch couple who owned many broad acres along the Raritan river, at Mapleton, in Middlesex county, New Jersey.[20] In his youth, Van Dyke had been a lieutenant of marines on board a privateer in the French and Indian War and at the outbreak of the Revolution had espoused the American cause.[21] Living then in New York City, he had raised a militia company called the "Granadiers," which was attached to Colonel John Lasher's First New York battalion. He and many of his men had been taken by the British on that disastrous September day in 1776, when Washington's army had fled in panic from Manhattan Island.[22] Elias Boudinot, American Commissary General of Prisoners who had visited New York under a flag of truce in 1778, reported that "Captain Vandyke had been confined 18 months for being concerned in setting fire to the City, when, on my calling for the Provost Books, it appeared that he had been made Prisoner & closely confined in the Provost 4 days before the fire happened." [23]

"He was treated with uncommon rigor during the whole time of a long captivity," Washington related to the Board of Admiralty, "owing, as is supposed, to the influence of those persons who remained voluntarily in the town, and to whom he was particularly obnoxious on account of his opposition to their measures from the commencement of the dispute. The little property he was possessed of fell into the hands of the enemy, and as no provision has been made for him, either in the Army or in the state, he had been reduced to a condition truly distressing." [24]

Thus, although sixty-one years old when assigned to the *Saratoga* as a lieutenant of marines, Van Dyke's experiences with the British gave promise of a savage fighter, and John Young was looking for fighters.

Of the background of the *Saratoga*'s surgeon, Dr. William Brown, of Philadelphia, the record reveals little. He may have been kin to the more famous medical man of the same name, who hailed from Virginia and who, while in the Surgeon General's department of the army, published the first American pharmacopoeia. [25] Save for the fact that young Dr. Brown looked upon a naval career as hazardous and, "considering the Uncertainty of this transitory Life," decided, on July 28, to make a will, we would have known even less about him. A brother, John Brown, and a cousin, Dr. Joseph Eaker, were named as beneficiaries. [26] In further recognition of the exigencies of the times, the naval surgeon the same day gave power of attorney to administer his affairs in his absence "to friend Robert Bailey, of Philadelphia, Shop keeper." [27]

From New Hampshire came the *Saratoga*'s sailing master, John Garvin. [28] In following the sea, he was treading in his father's footsteps, for James Garvin, who in 1780 was a prosperous merchant in Somersworth (now Rollinsford) New Hampshire, had come to America as a stowaway while a lad in his teens and had been a sea captain before settling to the most prosaic life of a trader in West India goods. [29] James Gar-

vin had married Sarah Hobbs of a New Hampshire
family, and John, their fifth child, was born May 12,
1757.[30] At the age of twenty he had enrolled as a seaman under John Paul Jones in the *Ranger,* had been a
member of the prize crew which brought in the
Drake,[31] and had risen to the rank of midshipman.[32]
Captured at Charleston in May, 1780, he had arrived
in Philadelphia on June 21, along with many other
officers liberated on parole.[33] His exchange had been
effected just in time for him to sign up with Young as
sailing master.

There were two master's mates, William Brown
Faggo of Boston and John Hackett of Philadelphia.
Research does not divulge much information on
Faggo, the senior master's mate—"My Billy," as his
widowed mother, Mary Faggo, called him.[34] He was
born February 6, 1759, and was therefore just a few
months in his majority when he joined the new sloop-
of-war.[35] It is apparent he had had considerable experience at sea, and from his letters it is also evident
he had received a good education.[36]

The second master's mate, John Hackett, had had
a checkered career. He was not as youthful as Faggo;
in fact, he was a widower with a small son, George,
who was then attending school and whose care he had
entrusted to a close personal friend, Colonel Thomas
Jones.[37] Colonel Jones attested warmly to his knowledge of "Mr. Hackett's attachment to the American
cause, and his stepping forth at an early period to its
defense."[38] Old records confirm the Colonel's knowledge. Hackett signed up as boatswain's mate in the
galley *Dickinson* in the Pennsylvania navy in 1775,[39]
and rose to be commissioned first lieutenant of the

galley *Ranger* the next year.[40] Unfortunately, an act
of insubordination in January, 1777, caused him to be
"broke by Court Martial."[41] Apparently he was willing to accept a master's mate warrant in the *Saratoga*
to regain his good name. He had chosen well, for his
commander, too, was out to win reputation anew.

The midshipmen, four in number, were as interesting a group of promising youngsters as ever gathered
in a junior mess: John Lawrence Livingston of New
Jersey, Barent Sebring of New York, Nathaniel Penfield of Connecticut, and Samuel Clarkson of Pennsylvania. Most of them were, as young Livingston's
father had said, "the children of respectable families,"
drawn to the sea by the lure of adventure and permitted by their parents to enter the naval service because educational institutions were closed during "a
period of general internal disorganization."[42]

Senior midshipman was Livingston, who celebrated
his eighteenth birthday on July 15, 1780, on board the
Saratoga.[43] It is likely that the youngster was exces-
sively bored by the tender solicitudes of his aged father, New Jersey's Governor, and of his two doting
sisters. The Misses Kitty and Susan Livingston were
summering in Philadelphia because of British activities around their home in northern New Jersey.
"Brother Jack has received a summons to his duty on
board the Saratoga, the ship being shortly to sail on a
cruise," Kitty reported by letter on July 10, to still a
third sister, Mrs. John Jay, wife of the American
Minister, who had finally reached his Spanish destination. "I hope the sea will rid him of the fever and ague
that has long been his Companion."[44]

It was of other companions than sickness, however,

that the old governor had thought when he sent his youngest lad into the naval service. In a memorable charge to his son at parting, he cautioned: "When you are obliged to associate with the common mariners, I would have you act towards them with becoming familiarity and freedom, without assuming any airs of superiority on account of your connections, but I would by no means have you enter into their vulgarisms and low-lived practises, for which they themselves will rather despise you; and above all, that you must carefully avoid contracting that abominable custom, so common among seamen, of profaning the name of God by oaths and imprecations."

Shore leave, young Livingston was told, should be regarded as an educational opportunity. "Whenever you lay in any port, inquire as you have time and opportunity into the following particulars respecting the country, viz—1, its soil and produce—2, manufactures and trade—3, government—4, curiosities—5, religion; but particularly into the principal articles of their imports, and their duties or customs on merchandize, and also what articles among them are prohibited or contraband. And enter the substance of all your information on the above heads, in a book kept for that purpose."

Against the mariner's traditional profligacy, the old Governor particularly warned his son:

I must press upon you to be saving of your money, and not to spend it unnecessarily. If you do not observe this direction, you will find by woeful experience that you have rejected the most salutary advice. From the diminution of my estate by the depreciation of the currency, you and your brothers must expect to make your fortunes by your own

industry and frugality. But when I advise you to be saving of
your money, I do not intend that you should ever appear mean
and niggardly, nor grudge little expense upon proper occa-
sions, when you must either part with your money or appear
contemptible; as when you are necessarily engaged in company, and they go rather farther in the expenses of the club
than you could wish; in such case and in others that will
occur, one must sometimes conform against his inclinations,
to save his character, and afterwards make it up by re-
trenching some other expenses and a greater economy.

Almost a sense of impending disaster seemed to
have influenced the benediction with which the Governor sent his son to his ship. "And now, my dear
child," he wrote, "I wish you a safe voyage with prosperity in this world, and everlasting happiness in the
next; and to secure the last, which is of infinitely the
greatest consequence, oh! let me entreat you not to
forget your Creator in the days of your youth, but
wherever you go, to remember your duty to the great
God, who alone can prosper you in this life, and make
you happy in that which is to come."[45]

To John Young's personal interest can be attrib-
uted the appointment of Midshipman Barent Sebring.
Sebring was his wife's first cousin, the fifth child of
her aunt Susanna Roome, who had married Barent
Sebring, Senior, in 1747. Born in August, 1756, young
Sebring's history is obscure until he arrived in Philadelphia in the summer of 1780 to assume his post on
board the *Saratoga*. His name (or that of his father,
for it is impossible to determine which) appears upon
various New York muster rolls of the Revolutionary
period, but his experiences at sea seem to have begun
under his cousin's husband.[46]

Midshipman Nathaniel Penfield came from Fairfield, Connecticut—the son of a family that stretched back four generations to a Samuel Penfield who had crossed from Wales to Massachusetts prior to 1679 and had been a pioneer settler in Rhode Island. A son, Peter, had founded the Penfield flour mills at Fairfield. A grandson, Samuel—Midshipman Penfield's father—fought in the French and Indian War and had been "out" as a lieutenant in the Continental line in 1776.[47] Young Nathaniel, born in 1759, apparently saw no naval service prior to joining the *Saratoga,* but he had sailed before. We come upon him first as one of the little group of midshipmen selected by John Young, and he quite evidently was a seasoned seaman.[48]

Midshipman Samuel Clarkson was the scion of a family prominent for generations in colonial history. His great-grandfather Matthew Clarkson had been secretary of the province of New York from 1689 to his death in 1702. His father, Dr. Gerardus Clarkson, was a noted Philadelphia physician and patriot. Samuel was his oldest child, born July 31, 1762,[49] and had been appointed an acting midshipman in the navy in the summer of 1779. At that time his father had aspired to secure for the lad a European education and had sent him abroad in the *Confederacy,* when she sailed with Gérard and John Jay. The Marine Committee had instructed Captain Harding "that Mr. Clarkson, an Acting Midshipman on board shall have leave to stay in France for his education."[50] Inasmuch as the *Confederacy* got no further than Martinique and returned from there to Philadelphia, Harding discharged the youngster as he already had a full quota of midshipmen. But for the remark of Kitty Livingston in one of her letters, we might have lost track of the lad at that point. Kitty, however, in telling of her brother's call to duty in the *Saratoga,* commented, "Sam Clarkson has a place in the same ship."[51] Clarkson reported on board on July 1.[52]

Enlisting a crew for the sloop-of-war and recruiting the personnel of the frigate *Confederacy* to proper strength did not at first glance present any difficulties to Francis Lewis, who knew that "an embargo is laid on by this state, and a considerable number of Seafaring men [are] in port."[53] He knew too that both vessels could draw from the small crew of the Continental sloop *West Florida,* which by Congressional action in June was to be sold and her men apportioned to other naval vessels.[54] The *West Florida* had arrived in port after participating in some stirring episodes of the war along the Gulf coast near New Orleans.[55]

Seamen were available, but they would not sign on. The Continental service, with its wages in Continental dollars, was no lure to a sailor who, once the embargo was lifted, could earn real specie on a privateer. The men from the *West Florida* were a nucleus, but the nucleus refused to grow. After two weeks of futile effort, John Young and Seth Harding went to the Board of Admiralty. They pointed out that the pay of officers and men "is now by Depreciation become so nearly reduced to nothing as to be Considered by Seamen as no reward for Pass'd services, or inducement to engage in the future."[56]

Lewis had received similar information from the Nicholson brothers in Boston. He took his troubles to Congress, on July 11, with a series of resolutions for their solution. These provided that pay for officers and men be hereafter in specie; that subsistence of officers be similarly reckoned; that a bounty of twenty dollars, one-half to be paid before sailing, be allowed every able-bodied seaman enlisting for a year, and ten dollars to every ordinary seaman or landsman; that forty Continental dollars be considered the equivalent of a dollar in specie, and that the resolution apply to the officers and men of the *Trumbull, Deane, Confederacy,* and *Saratoga.* Congress struck out "officers" and approved the wage and bounty provisions for the men only. It almost became more lucrative to serve before the mast than on the quarter deck.[57]

With a hard money incentive and a attractive bonus, John Young could cajole seamen into service. Of the former crew of the *West Florida,* the only surviving names on the *Saratoga*'s roster are those of Stephen Thompson, able seaman, and Anthony Castoff, "a Nagro Man" who "will pass for a seaman."[58] The Supreme Executive Council of Pennsylvania supplemented the personnel with a few convicts pardoned upon condition "that they enter on board the Saratoga . . . and serve during the present war."[59] Of those who shipped of their own volition, we have but a fragmentary list.[60] For the rest, we know only that, by the end of July, the *Saratoga* was "full of men."[61]

We know also that Young had his sloop-of-war "ready to fall down the river." But before he could sail, the crew that had been lured by higher wages would have to be paid the promised bounty. He went to the Board of Admiralty and found it "broke" as usual. The finances of the Navy Board of the Middle District were in even worse shape. The trouble was again referred to Congress, which on July 25, ordered a warrant issued on the treasurer in favor of the Board of Admiralty "for forty thousand dollars to enable them to advance a month's pay to the men belonging to the Saratoga sloop of war."[62]

CHAPTER V

The Strategy of Francis Lewis

THE French had come at last. The first division
arrived at Rhode Island on July 12, 1780, and
the Chevalier de la Luzerne, announcing the auspi-
cious event ten days later to Congress, was happy to
add that a second division was about to set sail for
America. For this latter news he again urged secrecy,
hoping the amiable legislators "will approve of this
reserve, both an account of the uncertainty of events
at sea, and because the enemy should be kept in ig-
norance of our measures."[1] On July 25, he presented
a sensible recommendation: the Continental frigates
should be assigned to the French squadron and placed
under the orders of the Chevalier de Ternay for combined naval operations. Tactfully, the Minister offered it only as a suggestion; he would not think of
pressing the matter, he indicated, were the frigates already destined for some other service.[2] Congress listened to the proposal and appointed a committee to
confer with him.[3]

We can appreciate how little this idea appealed to
Francis Lewis and his associates. The Board of Admiralty was just hitting its stride. It had four members now, two from Congress, who gave some attention

to naval matters when time permitted,[4] and two who
devoted every minute to the well-being of the navy.
One of these, of course, was the purposeful Chairman;
the other was William Ellery, of Rhode Island. Originally Ellery had been a Congressional member, but
since June, when his term in Congress had expired, he
had been an active Commissioner.[5] They had heard
recently from Boston; the *Trumbull* and *Deane* probably were on their way to the Delaware capes. The
dream of a joint cruise seemed at the point of realiza-
tion.[6] Yet they dared not ask the committee to insult
their allies with a deliberate rejection of the plan proposed by M. de la Luzerne. But a happy compromise
was effected and approved by Congress on July 26.
The frigates *Trumbull, Confederacy,* and *Deane* and
the sloop-of-war *Saratoga* were to "be put under the
direction of General Washington to be employed in
cooperating with the fleet of his Most Christian Majesty, commanded by Admiral the Chevalier de Ternay, in any naval enterprizes on the coasts of North
America."

How Washington, in northern New Jersey, could
intelligently command a sea force seemed beside the
point. M. de la Luzerne was further informed that the
Trumbull and *Deane* were expected in port "sometime in the next week" and, with the *Saratoga,* should
be able to join the French squadron by August 15.[7]
And the *Confederacy?* The estimated cost of fitting
her out was $973,736 in Continental money,[8] and
$700,000 was all Congress could promise just then for
every requirement of the Board of Admiralty.

Whatever intentions Congress had in placing the
Continental vessels under Washington, Francis Lewis'

interpretation was that the General's command would begin only when the fleets joined. With De Ternay already blockaded in Rhode Island by a superior British force, such juncture seemed remote. Hence, he proceeded blithely with his pet scheme, arguing that "we think it would be most conducive to the Public interest, and most Satisfactory to the Officers and men that they should be employed in cruizing." [9]

Certainly it was "most Satisfactory" to John Young. From February to August had been a long, grilling period, and once he had almost lost his ship. He wanted to get away before some new Congressional resolution might rob him of opportunity, and too he no doubt wanted to escape the unbearable heat wave which had engulfed Philadelphia in the first week of August. Even the prosaic newspapers took note of the weather, citing Sunday, August 6, as "the hottest day known for a number of years in this city." The thermometer had registered $84\frac{1}{2}°$, "and in one in the neighbourhood of this city it was as high as 98°." A Philadelphia diarist took note of it as "the hottest day in fifty-three years; since 1727." [10]

Between the urge for action and the heat, John Young was keyed to a "do or die" determination. On August 8, he made his will—a simple document, which he signed and which was witnessed by William Semple, his friend, and John Pringle, another Philadelphian with privateering instincts and inclinations. A printed form, designed especially for seafaring men, was used. The few additions made by the captain in this instrument are shown in italics:

I, *John Young of the City of Philadᵃ Mariner* considering the Uncertainty of this transitory Life, do make and declare

these Presents to contain my last Will and Testament: That
is to say, I give and bequeath unto *my loving Wife Joanna
Young* all my Estate, real and personal, wherewith at the
Time of my Decease I shall be possessed or invested, or which
shall belong or of right appertain unto me, I do give, devise
and bequeath unto *the said Joanna Young.* And I do hereby nominate and appoint *the said Joanna Young* to be *my*
Execut*rix* of this my last Will and Testament, hereby re-
voking all former Wills and Testaments by me made, and do
declare this to be my last. IN WITNESS whereof I have here-
unto set my Hand and Seal, this *eighth* Day of *August*
Annoque Domini One Thousand Seven Hundred and *Eighty*

Signed, Sealed, and Declared to be the last Will and Testament of h*im* the said *John Young*

Signed & Sealed in the Presence of

William Semple
John Pringle   *Jn⁰ Young*[11]

Thus, having provided for his wife should life indeed prove "transitory," the captain repaired to the
Board of Admiralty and learned that his orders were
being drawn up. He was to cruise—in company with
the *Trumbull* and *Deane* if they arrived at the capes
in time—but first, there was a convoy job in store for
him.

In the river was the Continental packet *Mercury,*
the fleetest craft in America, under command of William Pickles, late captain of the *West Florida.* The
Mercury was waiting to take to Europe the eminent
statesman and late president of Congress, Henry
Laurens, of South Carolina.[12] Ten months earlier Congress had commissioned Laurens to proceed to Holland and negotiate there a ten million dollar loan.[13]
The siege of Charleston had frustrated the envoy's

various efforts to sail from that southern port, and he
finally had arrived in Philadelphia, hoping for some
adequate conveyance from thence to his destination.[14]
To his previous instructions, Congress thereupon
added an injunction to find out on what terms Holland would enter into a treaty of commerce with the
United States,[15] and ordered thirty thousand dollars
paid to the Board of Admiralty "to procure sea stores
for the passage of the honble Henry Laurens."[16]

John Young received his orders from John Brown,
secretary of the Board of Admiralty, on August 11.
He was directed to drop down the river, take the
Mercury under convoy, and proceed to sea, giving her
"as good as Offing as you can consistent with your returning to the Capes in four or five days." In case the
Trumbull and *Deane* were encountered in the river or
lower bay, the captain was supplied with a letter to
Captain James Nicholson, who as senior officer would
assume command of the squadron. Should neither
frigate be at the capes, Young was to return from his
convoying and continue there, endeavoring meanwhile
to fish up the anchor the *Confederacy* had lost near
Cape Henlopen the previous April.[17] In the letter to
Nicholson were specific orders to take command, give
the *Mercury* a good offing, and then cruise with his
consorts "along and off this Coast" for a fortnight, returning thereafter to the capes and sending word to
the Board of "the State & condition of your ships and
their Stores."[18]

Hopeful as Lewis might be of a joint cruise, it is
apparent by the very definite instructions which comprised much of John Young's orders that the Chairman was none too optimistic about the arrival in time

of the *Trumbull* and *Deane*. Also, as this was the
initial cruise of the new sloop-of-war, Young was urged
to every proper precaution. He was to make immediate regulations for quartering his officers and men
and distributing them to the "great Guns, small Arms,
rigging, &c." He was to discipline the ship's company
at the batteries "to render them more expert in time
of Battle." He was to take great care of the powder
room "to prevent accidents from fire." He was to
husband the ship's stores and provisions and see that
there occurred no "misapplication or waste thereof."
He was, while at the capes, to catch fish, "which will
afford a healthful variety of food to [his] Crew, &
save [the] flesh Provisions." Finally, he was "directed
to observe frugality in the expenditure of Stores and
provisions, preserve good Order and discipline and ex-
ercise [his] men frequently and keep a healthful and
clean ship, & do every thing in [his] power becoming
the duty character and honor of a commander of a
Ship belonging to the United States of America."[19]

From M. de la Luzerne, Lewis had obtained a letter
to the officer commanding the second division of the
French fleet. This letter, too, was entrusted to Young,
with the thought that during his cruise he might encounter this expected reinforcement; if so, he could
give the French "intelligence of the situation of the
enemys fleet."[20]

George Washington, writing from headquarters on
August 6, was in accord with Lewis' belief that the
Continental vessels would not be under his direction
until there was a junction with the French fleet. He
wanted, however, to know if he was expected to take
any action before such a junction, "that I may govern

myself accordingly."[21] The Chairman of the Board of
Admiralty replied on August 14, in one lengthy,
breath-taking sentence:

We beg leave to inform you that the Continental Armed
Ship Saratoga John Young Commander went down the River
yesterday in Order to Convoy the Honble Henry Laurens Esq
in the Mercury Packet a few Leagues to sea, then to return
within the Capes, but should the Trumbull & Deane frigates
be arrived at the Capes (which is hourly expected) before her
Sailing, then Captain Young is directed to join those frigates
and to deliver our Orders to James Nicholson Esq Senior Captain, who is directed to cruize along this Coast with the Three
Ships so as to endeavour to fall in with the second Division
of the French Squadron and to give the commanding officers
intelligence of the situation of the enemys fleet and to return
to the Capes in fourteen days and there wait for further
orders.[22]

Lewis sent copies of Washington's letter and the
above reply to Congress, hoping the arrangements
made would "not be disagreeable" to them. Whether
or not it was intended that the General take charge "of
our little fleets before they had found a junction with
the fleet of our Ally" was left to "Congress to determine."

The Chairman of the Board of Admiralty had
watched the *Saratoga* drop down the river from Philadelphia on August 13 and was optimistic. Perhaps his
dream of a joint cruise was about to materialize. There
was one fly in the ointment—a "melancholy picture,"
which he reported to Congress. It was impossible to
proceed with any celerity in fitting the *Confederacy*
for sea; the Board had strained its credit "to the greatest stretch," and now the rope-maker had refused to

deliver the new cables for the frigate until he received
some money on account of the great debt owing him.
But that was not all. Provisions were needed; a large
sum of money would have to be advanced to induce
men to enlist; and "all the Money we have yet received from our warrant on the Treasury is only 7000
Dollars." It was too bad, but Congress, being also
without funds gave no answer to the appeal.[23]

These were the concerns of landsmen, however; the
Saratoga was away at last. Through the chevaux-de-
frise and past Chester she sailed; by nightfall she was
off Wilmington. Next day she dropped on down to
Reedy Island and thence to Port Penn, near Bombay
Hook, the *Mercury* packet in company. To John
Young, the familiar river and upper bay panorama
could not slip by too rapidly. He was straining to be
at sea, eager for action and for the opportunity to
give the public a better recollection of him than a
wrecked brig on Ocracoke Bar.

Of Port Penn, on the morning of August 15, they
sighted two large vessels coming up the bay—the
Trumbull and *Deane* at last. Young boarded the *Mercury* and conferred with Henry Laurens, while Captain Pickles signaled the approaching frigates to stand
by for a boat. Both ships hove to in the stream. Young
sent off the Board of Admiralty letter to James
Nicholson, and Laurens added a note asking the
Trumbull's captain to attend him on board the packet.
An answer came back promptly. Both frigates were
short of water. They would run up the bay, replenish
their supply, and return without delay. Laurens
watched them up sail and stand northward, a gloomy
look on his face.

"They will not return," was his doleful prediction to Young.

His pessimism, as he explained in after years, was because, "at that time little regard was paid to orders inconsistent with the captain's own convenience." And he was right. Four days of impatient waiting brought no word from the frigates. On the fourth day, Young and the South Carolinian talked it over. The wind was favorable, and as the captain pointed out, the equinoctial period with its storms was rapidly approaching. As a result, Laurens reported, "I ordered the sloop-of-war and the Mercury to prepare for sailing. We proceeded and went to sea the same day." It was August 18 when the *Saratoga* and her convoy slipped through the capes with no hostile ships around to molest them.[24]

Three days later, an express from Philadelphia rode into Lewes, Delaware. He bore a letter from the Board of Admiralty to Henry Fisher, Congress' faithful watchdog at Cape Henlopen, and a sealed packet for John Young. Fisher was directed to deliver the packet to the captain, as the *Saratoga* "will be at the Capes about the times this reaches your hands. . . . Your well known Zeal for your Country renders it unnecessary to say more than that the Speedy and safe delivery of these dispatches is of great importance to the Public."[25]

The contents of the packet, if delivered, could have changed the history of the last years of the Revolution. It contained an order to the Count de Guichen, commanding the French fleet at Santo Domingo, to dispatch immediately four ships of his command to reinforce De Ternay at Rhode Island. De Ternay had

suggested the *Saratoga* for the mission in a letter to
Washington on August 10, pointing out that if the
reinforcements arrived by the end of September, "I
could transport your Army to Long Island the beginning of October, and finally decide the fate of
America this year."[26] Washington had concurred and
forwarded the request to Congress. On August 19 that
body had directed the Board of Admiralty to "order
the Saratoga to sail immediately and to obey such
orders, and take charge of such despatches, as they
may receive from the committee of conference with the
Minister of France."[27]

Sensing the purpose behind this mysterious order,
Lewis saw opportunity to obey another Congressional
mandate of the previous June to send a Continental
vessel to Cap François for the stores in the hands of
Carabasse. He dashed off a letter to the French agent,
urging him to charter a fast-sailing vessel if the stores
could not be all shipped in the *Saratoga*.[28] In new
orders to John Young, he explained that the directions
to go to Cap François were being given upon "a Sup-
position that the Orders of the Committee will carry
you to or near Hispaniola, for your destination is to
us a profound Secret."[29]

Though he may have had all the zeal in the world,
Henry Fisher down at Lewes could not perform the
impossible. He reported by return of the express that
the *Saratoga* had already gone to sea. If she reappeared off the capes, he would deliver the packet per-
sonally. Meanwhile, he would hold it pending further
orders.

Assuming that Young would return to the Delaware at almost any moment, Lewis was content to let

matters rest that way. He had his hands full trying to rush the *Trumbull* and *Deane* to sea again. Why the Nicholsons had not gone back down the bay to join the Laurens convoy was evident in a report the Board of Admiralty made to Congress on August 19. The *Trumbull* "wants a considerable quantity of small rigging & stores," it was explained, while the *Deane* needed "sundry articles, together with fifty men to complete her Compliment, and both of them large quantities of bread to enable them to proceed on a Cruize." Now if Congress would just let the Board have two hundred thousand dollars of the seven hundred thousand authorized some time before, the two frigates could be ready for sea in eight or ten days, "which might be particularly advantageous at this time," as the British were not in a situation to afford much protection to the trade of New York.[30]

Lewis was well informed about the enemy. An appeal to all captains, merchant or privateer, had been made in the newspapers weekly during July and August to inform the Board of Admiralty "of the number, situation and movements of the enemy's ships of war in the West Indies, and other parts of North America."[31] By the information thus received, it was well known that the British admiral, Marriot Arbuthnot, was concentrating upon the French at Rhode Island, and was not safeguarding his lines of communication between New York and England, and New York and Charleston, South Carolina.

Here was a splendid opportunity, of course, but Congress, having read the Board of Admiralty report, took no further action than to refer it to the Board of Treasury. Francis Lewis and William Ellery fumed

for five days at the inaction and then took a bold step.
Ellery wrote the report, which went to Congress on
August 24. It began by stating that "the embarrass-
ments in which the public treasury and public boards
are involved for want of money have put the inven-
tion of this board to the torture to devise ways &
means to obtain a supply of that most necessary article [money]." They saw only one solution—employment of the Continental frigates in cruising between
New York and Charleston. Prizes were bound to be
made which might relieve the Board of Admiralty and
the Board of Treasury as well. After these prelimi-
naries, the Board of Admiralty became specific.

To promote this measure they ask the assistance of Congress,—they expect Congress to comply with their late request, that they would direct the Treasurer to pay two hundred thousand dollars on the warrant for seven hundred thousand, or otherwise to assist them in such a way as they might
judge will prove most effectual;—and particularly they request that Congress would prevent the continental vessels of
war being diverted from proceeding agreeably to the arrangements of the board without their being consulted, until cir-
cumstances shall render it practicable for them to cooperate
with the French squadron in such expeditions as Gen¹ Washington may have in contemplation.

This document, which certainly laid down the law
to the Congress, was read before that body the same
day. Perhaps none were more surprised at its reception than Lewis and Ellery. The question of the frigates going cruising was "left to the discretion of the
Admiralty."³² The Board's demand for money was
met by a confession. Congress had no two hundred
thousand dollars. Continental coffers were empty. The

best it could do was to order "a warrant to be paid out
of the first money that comes into the Treasury."[33]
And the Board's demand that it be consulted before
Continental vessels were ordered anywhere met with a
meek acceptance.[34]

By another severe strain on the Board of Admiralty's credit—perhaps with more "torture" than ever
before—Lewis managed to complete the two frigates'
outfits. He reported to Washington on August 31 that
Congress had ordered the *Saratoga* off with dispatches
under direction of a secret committee of conference
with the French minister and that John Young also
had orders to keep a good lookout for the second division of the French fleet. Reporting further upon the
status of the navy that Washington was supposed to
command, Lewis said he had ordered the *Trumbull*
and the *Deane* out on a cruise and that "the Confederacy is the only Continental frigate now in this Harbour but neither manned nor victualed for the Sea."[35]
So, on September 2, the Nicholson brothers sailed for
a three weeks' cruise, their complements brought up to
required strength by impressing between fifty and
sixty seamen from the *Fair American,* the *Holker,*
and the *General Greene,* privateers in the Delaware.[36]

Scarcely were the *Trumbull* and the *Deane* beyond
recall when Lewis learned that the packet for John
Young was still undelivered at Lewes. The *Saratoga*
had not reappeared. The Board of Admiralty chairman sent for it and damned Young for not obeying
orders. But Francis Lewis knew at heart that his own
precipitancy was at the bottom of the trouble. He had
assumed Washington would require no immediate
service from the Continental vessels and had dis-

patched the *Saratoga* without waiting to verify the assumption. To a certain extent, of course, he could blame Congress for this. Then, when the Commander in Chief had a mission for one vessel, it had been Lewis' bad luck to have sent that particular ship out of reach; and it had been his further misfortune to send off the two frigates when either could have been used for the secret mission.

As a result, the packet was not dispatched until September and by another conveyance; it did not reach Cap François until after De Guichen had sailed for home and was in a cipher for which the officer remaining on the station had not the key. Needless to say, reinforcements never arrived, and Carabasse still had his uncalled-for quantities of stores.[37]

CHAPTER VI

The First Cruise

THAT the packet whose contents might have changed the course of history lay uncalled for at the Delaware capes was through no fault of John Young. Charge it rather to Henry Laurens, who on that historic voyage made two mistakes—first, in detaining the *Saratoga* too long, and second, in discharging her too soon.

From the moment the *Saratoga* and the *Mercury* cleared the capes on the afternoon of August 18, a great discrepancy developed between the sailing abilities of the two vessels. John Young found his new sloop-of-war sluggish of movement, at least, in comparison with the fleet packet. The basic trouble he traced immediately to insufficient ballast.[1] The *Saratoga* was far from steady when under too heavy a spread of canvas. Frequently he was forced to shorten sail, and each time the *Mercury* drew far ahead so that by twilight she was several leagues in the lead. He came up with her only after dark, for Laurens, fearing to lose his convoy in the night, had ordered Captain Pickles to heave to.

The experience of the first day was repeated daily thereafter. Each night it became necessary for the packet to shorten sail, or the *Saratoga* would have been out of sight astern by dawn. Each morning Young tried every art of the experienced navigator to keep pace with the faster vessel but soon was hopelessly outdistanced. On the third night, he went aboard the *Mercury* to obtain Laurens' advice. Under orders of the Board of Admiralty to return to the Delaware capes "in four or five days," he felt the farce of escorting a ship that could sail rings around him had been about played out. To the envoy, he suggested that he had best turn back. But the latter did not agree. They were still uncomfortably near the American coast and hence, in danger of cruising British war vessels. Laurens wanted a better offing, although admitting that the *Saratoga's* slowness retarded their progress considerably. Would Captain Young please attend him several days longer? And that request, in which Young acquiesced, was Henry Laurens' first mistake.

We can imagine the mortification with which John Young returned from his conference and announced that the comedy would continue, and the chagrin of himself and his eager band of officers on each of the ensuing inglorious days. But an end came at last. On August 23, the sixth day of this farcical "convoy," Laurens finally felt himself far enough off the coast to release his escort. Presumably they had reached a point due south of Cape Sable. Again the captain was summoned to the *Mercury*.

"As we have been obliged to shorten sail every night, so that you could come up, much time has been lost," Laurens said. "Also I consider the Saratoga a very slender defence."

While John Young could offer no disclaimer to the

first part of the envoy's remarks, the disparagement of the sloop-of-war as a fighting force made him seeth inwardly. However, Laurens had no thought of being unkind, and hastened along to what he had in mind.

"May I recommend that you now make a short cruise and then return to the Delaware," he continued.[2]

Young accepted the proposal with alacrity, and Henry Laurens had made his second mistake.

Before they parted, the captain was entrusted with a brief letter to the Board of Admiralty. Possibly it contained an appreciation of his services, but the letter has not been found.[3] By noon, the *Saratoga,* on a southwesterly course, was hull down on the horizon, and the *Mercury* continued eastward with nothing now to retard her speed.

Onward the packet plowed through the Atlantic until, on the morning of September 3—at least a third of the voyage to Amsterdam behind her—she was sighted by the British frigate *Vestal.* That vessel, spying "a Brig or Brigantine or Vessel bearing or carrying a flagg or Colours with thirteen stripes and thirteen Starrs," promptly gave chase.[4] Captain William Pickles made a valiant effort to escape, but the *Vestal* was too swift. There could be no resistance, for the *Mercury*'s armament consisted of only four 4-pounders,[5] and her crew was comprised of the captain, two mates, boatswain, gunner, cook, nine seamen, and two black servants.[6] So she had to trust to her heels, and they were not speedy enough. The frigate began firing even before she came within range and discharged twelve guns before the *Mercury* hove to.[7]

Overboard, with iron shot to sink it, went the bag containing Mr. Laurens' papers. But alas! To the

envoy's extreme mortification, "the weight proved insufficient for the purpose intended,"[8] and the bag
floated. While Laurens was being hustled across to
face Captain George Keppel, of the *Vestal,* British
seamen fished it from the water, and all the damning
evidence fell into the enemy's hands. It is not surprising, therefore, that "On perusing said Papers it appeared to this Informant [Captain Keppel] that this
said Henry Laurens was authorized by the aforesaid
Preten[d] States of America to Negotiate a Loan and
to borrow a Sum Not exceeding ten Million Dollars
for the use of the said Pretended States of America.
Whereupon this Informant seized and detained the
said Henry Laurens."[9]

His report revealed the two mistakes. Had Laurens
dismissed the *Saratoga* on the third day as Young had
asked, by September 3 he would have been far beyond
the cruising ground of the *Vestal.* Had he retained
him longer than the sixth day, the slow progress would
have prevented Captain Keppel from sighting, on
that momentous September 3, a "Brig or Brigantine
or Vessel bearing or carrying a flagg or Colours with
thirteen stripes and thirteen Starrs." However, the
error of judgment that resulted in the capture of
Laurens was soon to draw Holland into a war where
Great Britain already had too many opponents.[10]

Between August 23 and September 9, the record is
silent regarding the *Saratoga*'s movements. John
Young was operating under conflicting orders. Lewis
had commanded his return to the Delaware capes in

at least five days. Laurens had made compliance impossible by detaining him six days and then recommending a cruise. Unquestionably, the captain found Laurens' instructions more to his inclination. So he cruised, and presumably he obeyed some of the injunctions of the Board of Admiralty in trying to whip his ship's company into shape by instilling discipline, and by exercising his gun crews at the 9- and 4-pounders. Undoubtedly also, he devoted no small part of his time to the *Saratoga*'s trim, shifting the scanty ballast, changing about stores and movable gear in the hold, and experimenting as to the spread of sail she could carry without danger of capsizing. From the meager evidence, his course after leaving the *Mercury* continued south by west, and consequently well offshore.

That he kept to the eastward of the cruising areas of enemy ships would indicate that he did not intend to risk his new sloop-of-war in any encounters until he had mastered her sailing vagaries and put his crew into some kind of fighting shape. But this we can only surmise and come to actual facts on the afternoon of September 9. By then, he had abandoned caution and was standing westward, athwart the coastal trade lanes about sixty leagues off the South Carolina coast. On that squally afternoon, a lookout in the top picked up a sail to the northwest. Young tacked, lowered his colors, and set out to investigate. Dusk was upon the sea before he drew near enough to make the quarry out. She was a brig, flying the British flag and apparently unperturbed by the pursuit.

They were in latitude 32° 10′ north, and longitude 76° 49′ west, and it was 8:30 P.M. when the *Saratoga*

drew abreast.[11] Gun crews were at their stations in
the dim glow of battle lanterns. The ship was cleared
for action and the air was surcharged with suspense.
Young hailed from the poop:

"What brig is that?"

The reply was made "Ingeniously," according to the
captain of the intercepted vessel:

"His Majesty's brig Keppel, John Steel, commanding; Charlestown for New York. Who are you?"

"This is the Continental sloop-of-war Saratoga,"
Young answered and at that instant the Stars and
Stripes began a jerky climb toward the peak. "Heave
to on our weather quarter or I open fire."

But Lieutenant Steel, courageous Britisher that he
was, had no such intention. As he could "think of no
other Expedient for the Safety of the Brigg under
my command," and as the *Saratoga* was on the starboard tack, he promptly veered athwart his enemy's
stern. Sensing the maneuver in its inception, Young
swung to port. At his sharp command, the 9-pounders
in the port battery flashed and roared in the night.
From the opponent came an answering broadside. The
enemy brig had not been caught napping.[12]

In the first few exchanges no harm appears to have
been done either vessel. It was quite evident to Young
that his gunners were not yet trained to their pieces,
particularly with a gale rapidly developing to stir up
an already choppy sea. As the deck lifted and dropped,
the gun nozzles seemed to point alternately into the
foaming water and then into the sky, with a jerky
brig visible only momentarily over the sights.[13] Resulted a deal of confusion on board and mighty little
precision to the firing.

Rather than waste ammunition in futile broadsides, Young determined to carry the brig by boarding. But here he had to reckon with both the weather and his lightly ballasted vessel. On the *Keppel,* they saw the boarders gathering and, noting that the *Saratoga* was "full of men," sheered off to a safe distance from the grappling irons.[14] The sloop-of-war had outsailed the brig in the long pursuit, but she could not outmaneuver her.

Again Young resorted to his guns, but the weather was too foul for the gun crews to master their weapons. The sloop-of-war's 9's and 4's were making a havoc of the brig's sails and rigging, but seldom indeed was a shot striking where it would do any serious damage.[15] Nor were the *Keppel's* sixteen 4-pounders being served with any better results. In fact, through the entire engagement, the *Saratoga* seems to have escaped with virtually no damage.[16]

A second attempt to board was as easily eluded by the enemy as had been the first effort. Thereafter Young continued the engagement at long range, apparently hoping that a chance shot might bring down a mast and cripple the brig. His gunfire did wound four of the British crew, one fatally. And twice 9-pound shot glanced from the *Keppel's* mainmast, but that was all. For six glasses (three hours), the battle raged. Then John Young gave it up as a bad job. At 11 P.M. he veered away and under a good press of canvas stood off before the wind, which was now blowing a hard gale.[17]

From such meager accounts as we have of this maiden testing of the *Saratoga,* the honors seem to rest largely with the enemy. The *Keppel* was armed only with 4-pounders, which should have been no match for the sloop-of-war's heavier metal. The British crew numbered fifty; the Americans, more than a hundred. To offset the advantages of weight or armament and larger complement, however, we know that the weather was unfavorable, that Young's hands were inexperienced and insufficiently trained, and that the *Saratoga's* lack of adequate ballast was a serious handicap.

Also, we have but a one-sided picture of his sea fight, and from British sources. No American version is extant; at least, none has been discovered. From Young's silence we would judge that he was unhappy over his failure to take the *Keppel,* and the evidence available does not show him in very brilliant colors. Upon Lieutenant Steel of the royal navy, however, there were honors to be bestowed. Reporting upon his arrival in New York on September 23, he said, "that the Master and Crew with the passengers behaved themselves as becometh the Character of Britons," adding that he had not attempted pursuit when the *Saratoga* drew off, as his sails and rigging were so damaged he "did not think it Expedient to Make Sail after her."[18] For his success in beating off the enemy, he was rewarded with a captaincy.[19]

Meantime John Young, after parting with the *Keppel,* stood directly for the Delaware capes. With little powder left in the magazine and the lockers almost empty of shot, the best place for the *Saratoga* was her home port. As the winds were kindly, the run was made in remarkably fast time, a further indication that only superficial damage, if any, could have been sustained in the three-hour engagement.

Good luck provided that Young should not return

from his first cruise empty-handed. When just a few
hours southeast of Cape Henlopen on the night of
September 12, he overtook a small snow-rigged British merchantman (a two masted, square-rigged, with
a trysail abaft the main mast). She was the *Sarah,*
Captain Allen McKinley, bound from Nevis for New
York and laden with 234 puncheons of West India
rum.[20] Being unarmed, she offered no resistance, and
Young was cheered by her rich cargo. Taking the
British master and hands on board the *Saratoga,* he
manned her with a prize crew and both vessels continued through the capes, arriving off Chester on the
afternoon of September 13. Strangely enough, in
recording the return of the sloop-of-war with her
prize, the newspapers made not a single reference to
the encounter with the *Keppel.*[21]

On September 12, in a most despondent mood,
Francis Lewis reported that "the admiralty are intirely destitute of Cash and so low is the present state
of the Treasury that although we have held a Warrant
dated the 5th August for 700,000 dollars, we cannot
yet obtain 200,000 to victual and man the Confederacy."[22] However, the news of Young's presence in
the river with a prize fired him with renewed enthusiasm. Here was complete confirmation of his avowal
before Congress that the best way to raise money was
to send the Continental ships cruising. He was sure
that "the Continental Moiety" of the *Sarah* would
complete the *Confederacy* at last. But, as Pennsylvania had prohibited public auctions, and the sale of
the cargo of rum privately would entail delay, he requested of Joseph Reed, President of the Pennsylvania Supreme Executive Council, permission to dis-

pose of it at public vendue, "as the speediest way to raise funds."[23] With rare promptness the Council resolved next day "that the same be granted."[24]

The *Sarah* and her precious rum were converted without delay into Continental dollars. She was libeled against September 19, condemned the next day,[25] and sold at noon of September 28 at the Coffee House. On that day also, the 234 puncheons of rum went under the hammer "on Mr. Willing's wharf."[26]

In his initial cruise, despite the inconclusive engagement with the *Keppel,* John Young had justified Lewis' refusal to dispose of the *Saratoga* and apply her sale price to outfitting the *Confederacy.* The Continental share of the proceeds of prize and cargo was the equivalent of what might have been realized for the sloop-of-war at public sale. Money was now available to get the *Confederacy* to sea, and the *Saratoga,* under Young's command, was still on the naval list for further services.

Humorously enough, in New York, Tory printer James Rivington jubilantly informed his readers on September 13 that "The Congress have sold the Ship Confederacy, one of their few remaining frigates, to the merchants of Philadelphia; the produce of the sale was intended to be applied for the raising men to augment their South Carolina army, now totally routed and annihilated by Lord Cornwallis."[27] The last phrase was unfortunately true. General Horatio Gates had lost his army and his reputation at Camden, South Carolina, on August 16, not quite a month before.[28]

CHAPTER VII

The Sea-Fighter

JOHN YOUNG came up from Chester to Philadelphia on the afternoon of September 13 to find Francis Lewis in a mood of rare exuberance. The arrival of the prize *Sarah* had been positively providential. Mentally he challenged anyone in Congress to question now the efficacy of measures proposed by the Board of Admiralty. And once more, the optimistic Chairman was off on his old hobby—a joint cruise. Not only could the *Confederacy* be completed, but the *Alliance,* which he had learned the week before had reached Boston from Europe, also could take part. True, all reports spoke of the disgraceful conditions on board, but John Barry had been ordered to take command of her,[1] and he would put her in shape by the time the *Confederacy* was ready for sea.[2] To make certain of this, Commissioner William Ellery had set off from Philadelphia on September 10. He would soon be on the spot for consultation "on the requisites necessary" for outfitting her with all possible dispatch.[3]

Francis Lewis once more was seeing things through roseate spectacles. He and Washington had reached a mutual understanding on employment of Continental vessels, which was in harmony with the opinion he had voiced to Congress in mid-August. De Ternay had made the suggestion to the American Commander in Chief that until there should be allied sea supremacy, the Continental frigates could best serve by cruising "to intercept the vessels which go from Charlestown to New York." Cruising was what the *Trumbull* and the *Deane* already were doing, and the Board of Admiralty chairman could visualize five American ships-of-war, in concert, sweeping the coast while all the more powerful British ships of the line and frigates were blockading the French in Rhode Island.[4]

"How soon can you again proceed to sea?" he asked Young as soon as the latter had made a detailed report of his first cruise.

"As soon as I can get additional ballast and replenish my ammunition," Young replied.

The matter of ballast presented an obstacle until the Navy Board of the Middle District recalled that more than a year before the Marine Committee had loaned twenty tons of iron ballast for the use of the Pennsylvania state ship *General Greene,* and that it had never been returned.

"Get it back at once," Lewis directed.

Then he dismissed Young with instructions to report on the morrow for sailing orders. By that time the question of ballast would be solved. No doubt the captain spent that night in the comfort of his Laurel street home, and on the morning of September 14 he presented himself again at the office of the Board of Admiralty. The Navy Board had learned there was a quantity of pig iron in one of the state galleys. Would that do as well as the broken cannon usually used as ballast, and how much was needed? Young thought the pig iron would do better, and estimated his re-

quirements as eight tons. Whereupon, the Navy
Board indited a formal request for that amount, and
dispatched it to Joseph Reed, President of the Pennsylvania Supreme Executive Council.[5]

Meantime, sailing orders in the neat hand of Secretary Brown were ready. They directed a cruise between Sandy Hook and Charleston, "or any other
part of the Coast which you may judge will be most
suitable for Annoying the trade of the enemy." Young
was to endeavor to join the *Trumbull* and the *Deane*
and to act in concert with them, but if these frigates
returned to port before his provisions were expended,
he should continue his cruise. Prizes preferably should
be sent into the Delaware, and Young, when the cruise
was completed, should run up the river to Chester,
and advise the Board of Admiralty of "the state and
condition of your ship." A close lookout for the expected second division of the French fleet was to be
maintained, so these hoped-for reinforcements could
be advised "of the number and situation of the British
fleet off Rhode Island." To facilitate communication,
M. de Ternay had adopted Continental signals, except that "those who have not an American flag will
hoist a Dutch one in the room of it at the same Mast."[6]

A letter to James Nicholson of the *Trumbull*, directing him to prolong the cruise of the two frigates,
was given Young before he set out for Chester. As a
little prodding to get results from the Nicholsons,
Lewis had included in this letter a sentence stating,
that "Captain Young of the Saratoga brought in yesterday a Prize Snow with 234 Puncheons of Rum &
he is ordered to proceed with his Ship immediately to
Sea and endeavour to join you."[7]

One of the Pennsylvania row-galleys came down
the river next day to deliver eight tons of pig iron, according to orders, to the sloop-of-war.[8] Young stowed
it below, properly ballasted at last. As the Navy Board
was prompt with powder and shot, he was ready to sail
by September 16. But first, he took steps to rid himself of four seamen, members of the crew of the snow
Sarah, who had refused to be won over to the Continental service. "No good oppertunity offering to send
the prisoners by water," he reported to the Navy
Board, "I have put them into Chester Jail untill some
safe conveyance offers to send them to Philadelphia
which you will please to inform the commissary [of
prisoners] of."[9]

With this final note to the Navy Board, just three
days after he had sailed up to Chester, Young headed
the *Saratoga* downstream.

This second cruise in the *Saratoga* began in one of
the gloomiest of the many disheartening periods which
frequently punctuated the protracted course of the
American Revolution. When Horatio Gates's military bubble had burst in the Carolinas, it had added
final disaster to a luckless southern campaign, which
had opened with the loss of Charleston. Around New
York a stalemate existed; Washington was too weak
to attack, and his French allies were bottled up in
Narragansett Bay. And the culminating military blow
—Benedict Arnold's treason at West Point—was
upon the eve of disclosure.

Spelling more immediate danger to John Young
was a sudden shift in the naval situation of which he
had no inkling. No longer were the ship lanes between New York and Charleston unguarded. George

Brydges Rodney, commander of His Majesty's forces
in the West Indies, unexpectedly had transferred his
base to New York, arriving there on September 15
with ten ships of the line and a number of frigates.
Since the hurricane season was approaching in the
tropics with its consequent danger to copper-bottomed
ships, and since all chances of naval operations in
southern waters were at an end for several months,
Rodney had sped northward to aid Arbuthnot in dis-
posing of M. de Ternay.[10] Sweeping along the southern coast, he had noted the unguarded sea lanes and
had detached two frigates off Charleston,[11] and two
more, the *Triton* and the *Guadaloupe,* off Virginia.[12]
And, further, immediately upon his arrival at New
York, he had begun preparations to send a formidable
squadron to cruise between Sandy Hook and Cape
Henry.[13]

John Young, when he cleared the Delaware capes
on September 18, was sailing forth into what was
shortly to become a hornet's nest. Inquiries at Lewes,
Delaware, had given him no information about the
Trumbull and the *Deane.* Neither had been reported
since they had sailed out earlier in the month. It was
a moot question where he would find them, if he found
them at all. He elected to cruise first to the northward,
up off the Jersey coast toward New York. At that
time both Continental frigates were operating around
Cape Hatteras and were ready to turn back to Philadelphia, "without taking anything worth naming."[14]
Helm to starboard might have brought about such a
joint cruise as Lewis had hoped for. Helm to port,
however, as the sloop-of-war nosed northward, removed every possibility of a junction. The letter to

James Nicholson was destined to repose undelivered in John Young's sea chest.

There was ease and smoothness in every movement of the *Saratoga* through the water. The additional ballast, properly stowed, had turned the trick. Satisfied with her sailing qualities, the captain turned his attention to the crew. The record of how he trained his hands is written only in subsequent results, but it is safe to assume no body of seamen ever received such intensive drilling in so short a time as John Young gave his crew in those late September days—teaching them the handling of 9- and 4-pound carriage guns, in fair weather or foul. The affair with the *Keppel* was a lesson he would not forget.

Southeast of the Jersey highlands, on September 25, the proficiency of one gun crew was tested. A small sloop, scampering for Sandy Hook and safety, was intercepted and brought to by a 4-pound shot laid neatly across her bow. She was the *Elizabeth,* of sixty tons burden, laden with Indian corn and spars.[15] Formerly American property, she had been taken several weeks before in Chesapeake Bay by a British privateer, the *Restoration,* Captain Hewes Burton. At the same time, Burton had destroyed an unfinished brig, removed her spars "and many other Articles," and loaded them in the *Elizabeth*. A prize crew then had essayed to sail the sloop to New York and had almost succeeded when the *Saratoga* happened upon her, and John Young changed her destination. A Tory New York newspaper on October 2 told its readers of the capture of the *Elizabeth* by Captain Burton, who "ordered her for this port but she is not arrived and 'tis feared is fallen into the hands of the enemy."[16]

Well-grounded fears, indeed, for, before that time, a prizemaster from the *Saratoga* had delivered the sloop to the Continental agent in Philadelphia, and a libel had been published on Young's behalf against the vessel, her cargo, and the three Negro slaves found on board her.[17]

While venturing no nearer New York than the point where he had taken the sloop *Elizabeth,* Young hovered in those waters for several days. Theoretically it should have proved good cruising ground; practically it did not. About the end of September, he turned his bow southward, sailing on a course paralleling the Jersey shore, but well to sea. Luck seemed to have deserted him. Since the recapture of the sloop, there had been no sign of further prey. The coastal waters off New Jersey and Delaware, usually a profitable hunting ground, were destitute of sail. Days were monotonous, but as each passed, Young felt growing confidence in the caliber of his ship's company. He was molding a crew which, given the opportunity, would show how a ship should be fought. And all unknown to him, those tranquil waters would soon lose their peaceful aspect, for, out past Sandy Hook on October 2, "Nine frigates and a number of armed vessels sailed on a cruise to the southward, to chastize the insolence of the rebel privateers, and protect the trade . . . from Gallic interlopers, so that it is now reasonable to imagine that very few vessels can either approach or go out from any port between [Charleston] and Sandy Hook, without permission from the commanders of his Majesty's ships." So announced the Tory press.[18]

Rodney had acted as he had planned. The squadron

which was to sweep the Atlantic coast actually consisted of four ships-of-the-line (the *Triumph,* the *Terrible,* the *Alcide,* and the *Intrepid*), and five frigates
(the *Cyclops,* the *Boreas,* the *Greyhound,* the *Raleigh,*
and the *Iris*).[19] It was an overwhelming force to un-
leash upon an unsuspecting little sloop-of-war. But
the elements were in league this time with John
Young. The uniformly fair weather which had ushered
in the month of October gave way to dark and over-
cast days, culminating on October 7, in a terrific storm
which lashed the length and breadth of the North
Atlantic coast.[20] It played havoc with the British
squadron. The seventy-four gun ship *Terrible* and the
frigate *Cyclops* lost their mizzenmasts and, badly
crippled, crawled back to port.[21] Farther south, the
Triton and the *Guadaloupe,* coming up the coast,
caught the full fury of the gale. Only by throwing
overboard eight 9-pounders did the *Guadaloupe* man-
age to keep afloat, and these two vessels abandoned
cruising to seek haven in New York.[22] But there remained at sea enough ships-of-the-line and frigates to
make it decidedly perilous for the *Saratoga.*[23]

During that gale of October 7, the well-ballasted
sloop-of-war ran southward before the wind, all sails
furled. John Young reveled in her performance.
When the storm passed—and it was as short as it was
violent—he found that only superficial damage had
been sustained. They had to fish the bowsprit and stop
some minor leaks with oakum.[24] Otherwise she was
sound as a bell. A reckoning in the late afternoon disclosed their position as about ten leagues east by south
of Cape Henry. If there was to be more stormy
weather, the captain did not want to encounter it off

Hatteras. Therefore, toward dusk, he ordered the helm about. They had come better than fifty leagues from the Jersey headlands without spotting an enemy craft. Perhaps there would be better luck cruising northward.

Dawn of October 8, a cloudy fall day with a good wind blowing,[25] disclosed two distant sail in the northwest quarter off the port bow. Through his glass, John Young made them out to be a fairly large ship and a small sloop. With recollections of the *Keppel* in mind, the captain sent a quartermaster to the flag locker for a British ensign, and, before starting in pursuit, hoisted the Union Jack instead of the Stars and Stripes—"a common and justifiable stratagem," to quote a writer of the time.[26] They were then about due east of Cape Henry.[27] As the *Saratoga* bowled nearer, it was apparent that they were not dealing with British naval vessels. The vessel looked like a heavily laden and well-armed letter-of-marque ship. The sloop was too small to require any serious consideration.

When but a short distance astern and coming up rapidly, Young sent his crew quietly to quarters, and Lieutenant Barney mustered a boarding party of fifty men who concealed themselves amidships. While the English flag seemed to have lulled any suspicions, the captain was taking no chances, particularly as he could count eleven muzzles protruding from the gunports of the big merchantman. Then the *Saratoga* pushed her nose into the open water between the two vessels, the ship to starboard, the sloop to port. The first hail came from the ship, her master suddenly alarmed at what seemed an ominously quiet approach.

"What ship is that?" was his anxious-voiced call.

"The Continental sloop-of-war *Saratoga*," Young replied. "Heave to, or I'll sink you!"

Even as the startled Britisher ordered a belated call to quarters, the Union Jack came tumbling down, and her true colors rose to the *Saratoga*'s peak. Young shouted a sharp command to his starboard battery. Eight 9-pounders spoke simultaneously, and the solid shot went crashing into the merchantman. In the pall of powder smoke, and before the reverberations of the deadly discharge had ceased, the sloop-of-war's helm was jammed hard to starboard, and she swept alongside her dazed opponent. Grappling irons, swung by practised hands, caught the running gear of the ship as they fouled. Barney and his fifty boarders rose from concealment with howls of excitement and went leaping, climbing, sprawling over the locked gunwales and spewed forth upon the enemy's deck. They were met by such Britishers as were not still befuddled by the surprise attack. There was a brief, bloody melee, but the impetuous dash of Barney and his men swept all opposition away.[28] Within ten minutes the deck was cleared, the flag hauled down, and a chagrined British seadog, Captain Robert Gill, of the letter-of-marque ship *Charming Molly,* Jamaica to New York, had surrendered his ship formally to John Young.[29]

The *Charming Molly* was indeed a prize, for she had a rich cargo of rum and sugar, boasted an armament of twenty-two 6-pounders, and carried a complement of ninety men. But for the ruse Young had employed, she could have given him a battle royal, whereas so complete had been the surprise that not a single 6-pounder had been touched off.[30]

Almost as quickly as he had taken the ship, the captain drew off the captured crew, leaving Barney on board as prizemaster with a prize crew of eight men.[31] There was still more prey to be had—the little sloop, which was scudding eastward like a frightened duck. The *Saratoga* was upon her like a hawk, and her flag came down with no thought of resistance. She was the *Two Brothers,* Captain Deane, also from Jamaica, and she carried a cargo of rum and sugar. A prizemaster boarded her, transferred her few hands to the sloop-of-war, and turned her bow northwestward for the distant Delaware.[32]

Night had fallen by the time they parted from the *Two Brothers.* Meanwhile, interrogation of the prisoners had disclosed the presence of more Jamaica-men in the vicinity. There had been five vessels in the fleet until they had been scattered by the storm of the day before. Somewhere in the neighboring dark waters were another heavily armed ship and two large brigs. Before he could determine his future course, the sound of minute guns—distress signals—indicated all was not well on board the prize ship. Ordering the helm about, Young stood westward and, toward midnight, was within hailing distance of the *Charming Molly.* Barney reported five feet of water in the hold, with the sea pouring in faster than the pumps could discharge it. One of the *Saratoga's* 9-pounders had sent a shot into the hull between wind and water. The sloop-of-war's carpenter was sent aboard to make temporary repairs, Young standing by until his return.

Before dawn, after instructing Barney to make for the Chesapeake rather than the Delaware because

of the crippled condition of the *Charming Molly,*
Young turned his bow into the northwest and resumed
the cruise.[33] With daybreak of October 9, he ordered
extra vigilance in the tops. He was after big prey.
One of the prisoners had given him much information
about the three vessels he was seeking. The ship was
called the *Elizabeth,* and carried twenty-eight 9- and
6-pounders. One of the brigs, the *Nancy,* boasted
fourteen 4-pounders; the other, the *Phoenix,* was but
indifferently armed. The captain would have been justified in giving over any thought of attempting to find
them. The *Saratoga's* armament was no match for
the ship; her complement was reduced by about twenty
men sent off in prize crews; her first lieutenant was
also on a prize; and the prisoners in the hold outnum-
bered the American hands. But John Young dis-
counted the odds against him. He had felt the keen
taste of victory. His crew had stood the test in the
engagement with the *Charming Molly.* The guns had
been served with lethal accuracy. He knew he had a
ship full of fighters. They and he were in a frame of
mind to have tackled a frigate.

The weather had cleared and visibility was good,
but scan the horizon as they might, the lookouts found
no sail to report. By nightfall, they were within a few
leagues of Cape Henlopen, and Young concluded
they must have overrun the quarry. That night he
stood eastward and, at dawn on October 10, a good
ten leagues from the land, he veered to the south. Just
before noon, with observations showing them to be
in latitude 38° 16′ north, a man in the top picked up
three sails dead ahead.[34] An hour later Young could
make them out through his glass—a ship and two

brigs—the rest of the Jamaica fleet. It was apparent, too, that they stood in no awe of the approaching sloop-of-war. They did not alter their northward course in the least.

Considering the odds against him, the captain would have been thoroughly warranted, according to the naval code of the time, to have resorted again to the ruse of false colors. What had worked so successfully with the *Charming Molly* and the *Two Brothers* stood similar chances of duping the *Elizabeth,* the *Nancy,* and the *Phoenix.* But he disdained the opportunity. This time the *Saratoga* was going into the fight under her true colors, and it was with the Stars and Stripes whipping in the breeze that she bowled down upon the enemy vessels.[35] The boatswain's whistle piped the crew to quarters, and Young steered a course that would carry him between the ship and one of the brigs.

No hails were interchanged. This was grim business with no thoughts of parley on either side. Approaching on opposite courses, they were abreast, the ship to port, the larger brig to starboard, before the first broadsides were exchanged. All three vessels fired simultaneously. Little damage was done to the *Saratoga,* but her starboard guns, discharged with telling effect, put the brig out of commission with that single broadside.

Then the trim sloop-of-war emerged from the powder smoke astern of the enemy. John Young saw the situation at a glance. The brig was done for. Disregarding her thereafter, he swung the *Saratoga* in a short arc to port. From that position, he raked the ship. Back on another tack and sailing rings around his lumbering opponent, he brought his starboard battery to bear, and the gunners, who had previously eliminated the brig, poured the third broadside into the ship. The return fire was high, damaging sails and shrouds only. And the ship, too, was now in distress. That was apparent to every eye on the sloop-of-war as they swung down upon her again. Before they could lash her with a fourth broadside, the British ensign came fluttering to the deck. The engagement had taken but two glasses—a scant hour.[36]

To the eastward, the remaining brig was fleeing down the wind. The captain decided to let her go. He had enough on his hands right then to keep him busy.[37] He ran down first alongside the ship and sent Master's Mate Hackett as prizemaster and Midshipman Clarkson as his mate, with instructions to send back the prisoners as quickly as possible and then stand for the Delaware capes.[38] Captain David Taylor, of the *Elizabeth,* came on board the Saratoga in the first boatload and confirmed all that Young had heard before. The ship mounted twenty-eight guns all right, had a crew of one hundred men, and carried several passengers and a cargo of rum and sugar.[39] She had a heavy casualty list as well, but the records as to the number of dead and wounded are missing.

Once the prisoners were confined below, Young turned his attention to the brig, which wallowed in the water some distance astern and to the westward. She was the *Nancy,* the one with the fourteen 4-pounders; the brig that had escaped was thus identified as the *Phoenix.* Sailing Master Garvin and a prize crew attended to the necessary repairs, while Captain Oswald Eve, of the *Nancy,* several passengers, and thirty hands were sent on board the *Saratoga.*[40] Like her consorts', her cargo consisted of rum and sugar. Just at twilight, she got under sail for the Delaware.

John Young was about to follow her with the *Saratoga* when signal guns were heard from the *Elizabeth*. Seeing that the prize ship was slowly coming up, the sloop-of-war's top sails were hove to the masts and her arrival awaited. Hackett reported a situation almost identical with the experience of the *Charming Molly*. The *Elizabeth* had been hulled several times between wind and water and much of her rigging had been shot away. After he had "got matters Put to rights," Hackett had stood after the *Saratoga* but had found the ship very loggish, which "seemed to bring her chain plates near the water." He put both pumps to work, but they refused to suck, so he drew the pump boxes, sounded, and learned he had eight feet of water in the hold. It was then he had signaled for help.

From the *Saratoga* they could see where the *Elizabeth* was making water. Young put the carpenter on board with plugs to stop the hole.[41] He also sent his first master's mate, William Brown Faggo, to take over the command from Hackett, and increased the size of the prize crew to forty-two men. This unusual number of hands to man the ship indicates clearly how highly he valued her.[42] Hackett resented being superseded, fearing a "doubtful opinion" of him on Young's part, but it is more likely that the captain felt the ship's condition warranted putting a more experienced officer in charge. What made it hard for Hackett to accept was the fact that Faggo was "a youngster."[43]

Leaving the *Elizabeth* to make the best of her way for port, the *Saratoga* set sail about midnight on a due northerly course and, with dawn, was once more drawing close to Cape Henlopen. Daybreak disclosed two sails, one directly over the bow and about two leagues distant; the other, far to the northwest. The captain was concerned about them. They might prove barriers to the entrance to the Delaware for both himself and his prizes. For once, he became cautious, studying them through his glass, and maintaining his original course. By seven o'clock, he had approached to a point where he could make them out clearly. One long last look and he turned to Lieutenant Allison.

"The sail to the northwestward is a ship-of-the-line," he said. "The one dead ahead is a merchant brig. They're about two leagues apart, and I'm going to snatch that brig right under the Britisher's nose."[44]

It was an audacious determination and was carried out with the same verve and dash that had marked the entire cruise. The fleet sloop-of-war, under every stitch of canvas she could carry, fairly leaped through the water. Ahead of her, the brig, suddenly alarmed, veered to starboard, away from the protection of the man-of-war. Within an hour she was overhauled, and Young one eye on the distant ship of the line and the other on his quarry, called across the water:

"Heave to, or I'll sink you! What brig is that?"

Sails on the vessel came down on the run, as a voice answered:

"We surrender. This is the brig *Providence,* a prize, bound for New York."[45]

Young sent Midshipman Penfield and six men on board, instructing the former: "Work fast. We'll have the man-of-war on our heels any minute."

Penfield followed his orders. The British prize crew

—a midshipman, a mate, and six seamen—were sent
back to the *Saratoga* in the returning longboat, and
by the time the boat was hoisted in the brig had made
sail.[46] It was high time, for the big Britisher to leeward—she was the seventy-four gun ship *Alcide* of
Rodney's cruising squadron—had at last gotten wind
of something suspicious happening under her nose
and was coming down under a great spread of canvas.
The brig ran straight eastward; the *Saratoga* to the
north. Which scurrying sail would the enemy pursue?
The Honorable Walter Young, commanding the
Alcide, elected to take after the brig.[47]

John Young could have wished it otherwise. He
had every confidence that the *Saratoga* could have
outsailed the pursuer. Meanwhile, from Midshipman
William Thackstone, of His Majesty's frigate *Triton,*
and William Grindley, master's mate of His Majesty's frigate *Guadaloupe,* the two British prize-
masters, the captain learned something about his
latest prize.[48] She had been the American brig *Providence,* of ninety tons burden, Captain Samuel Young,
bound from Port-au-Prince to Philadelphia with a
cargo of sugar and coffee, and had been captured on
October 2, by the *Triton* and the *Guadaloupe* when
some fifty leagues southeast of Cape Henry.[49] Her
master and six hands had been removed, and a joint
prize crew sent on board from the two frigates. Thackstone and Grindley had been disturbed that morning
when they sighted a sail near Cape Henlopen. They
could not make her out and were afraid to venture
too near. So intent had they been on this possible
enemy that they had failed to see the *Saratoga* until
she was almost upon them.[50]

John Young heard their story and leveled his glass on the distant vessels. The ship of the line was gaining hand over hand upon the brig. Mentally, the captain crossed the *Providence* off his prize list. Now it behooved him to consider his own situation. He had not expected to find any heavy British vessels in the waters around the Delaware capes. Yet, if one was there, possibly others were not far off. His crew mustered less than fifty men. The rest were away on prizes. Under hatches he had more than two hundred prisoners. Ammunition was about exhausted. He had succeeded beyond his fondest expectations. Thanks to the pursuit stretching away to the eastward, the way to the Delaware was clear. Prudence dictated his return to port. So, he turned the *Saratoga*'s bow westward and, one day later, nosed through the capes and stood up the bay.[51]

CHAPTER VIII

Prizes and Prisoners

A midshipman astride a jaded nag pulled up before the Board of Admiralty office in William West's house on Front street around noon of October 14, alighted with a sigh of relief—a thirty-mile jaunt ended—twisted the reins about a convenient hitching post, and entered the Board's sanctum. Two gentlemen, Mr. Commissioner Lewis and Mr. Secretary Brown, glanced up with a preoccupied air from a paper-ladened table. The midshipman saluted, extended a letter, and spoke:

"From Captain Young, Sir. The *Saratoga* is off Chester, and the captain desires immediate advice as to his prisoners. There are better than two hundred of them."

Francis Lewis emitted a gasp of astonishment, grabbed the extended letter, and, for a few tense moments, absorbed its contents, Secretary Brown leaning forward to read over his shoulder. The momentous tidings leaped from the pages . . . anchored off Chester at dawn . . . a successful cruise . . . six valuable prizes including three heavily armed merchantmen . . . about two hundred and twenty prisoners on board . . . prizes expected any hour . . . the *Saratoga* in need of some repairs . . . directions from the Board of Admiralty desired at once. With an exclamation of unalloyed happiness, Lewis sprang into action.

"Magnificent!" he cried. "A glass of Madeira for the young gentleman, Mr. Brown."

The Commissioner and the Secretary set speedily to work. Notification went off to the Deputy Commissary of Prisoners to prepare to handle several hundred more men in the new jail. A letter was dispatched by express to Young, asking for a complete return of prisoners and instructing him to land them at Chester and report his detailed needs. To the Navy Board of the Middle District went instructions to send carpenters down to Chester, to arrange to revictual the *Saratoga,* and to apply to the Commissary for ammunition and powder.[1] Francis Lewis intended to see to it that if humanly and financially possible, there would be no delay in sending the *Saratoga* out again. John Young was one captain who did not return empty-handed.

Right from the heart came Lewis' approval of the captain's enterprise. The *Trumbull* and the *Deane* had ascended the river to Chester a week before, after a three-week cruise which had resulted in the capture of but two coastal vessels, only one of which had reached port. The two frigates had returned from the cruise, as a midshipman on the *Deane* remarked, "without having taken anything worth naming, which is a great disappointment to the Admiralty Board." By contrast, the accomplishments of the sloop-of-war were phenomenal. Now *Trumbull, Deane,* and *Saratoga* lay at Chester, with no money to outfit them. Lewis was beginning to agree with the opinion of seafaring men that the distance from Philadelphia to

the Delaware capes, and the difficulties of the navigation of the bay and river rendered the capital city
"entirely unfit for the reception of ships of war." That
was why he held them at Chester, which was thirty
miles nearer the sea.[2]

While Secretary Brown's quill scratched out the
necessary epistles, Lewis questioned the midshipman,
learning the details of that surprising cruise. Others
who came in listened, too, and before long the news
was passing from mouth to mouth throughout the city.

Miss Susan Livingston heard it and penned a letter
to her sister in Spain. Their beloved brother Johnny
was safe at Chester. The *Saratoga* had taken three
letter-of-marque ships of considerable force and laden
with rum and sugar. Susan speculated upon the mone-
tary reward which would be coming to Midshipman
Livingston: "As the officers and men are entitled to
one half the prizes, and a midshipman has three shares,
it is supposed that Johnny's share will amount to near
twenty thousand pounds."

Not only was Miss Susan counting her brother's
chickens before they were hatched, however; she was
also figuring in Continental currency.[3]

Down at Chester on the afternoon of October 14,
John Young was doing some counting, too, but in
terms of British tars. Militia officers were taking the
prisoners off his hands, and he was tabulating an exact
return. First to be handed into custody were the captured officers and passengers. There were four masters, four passengers, two midshipmen of the British
navy, and more than a dozen mates and petty officers.[4]
These with some two hundred seamen were all ashore
and marching northward under guard before night-

fall.[5] Thomas Bradford, Deputy Commissary of
Prisoners, welcomed them, figuratively speaking, with
open arms. Exchange of naval prisoners from New
York had been woefully hampered in past months by
lack of American prizetaking. Exchange, like a mercantile transaction, was on a ledger basis, and Young
had pretty well balanced the ledger in a single cruise.
Hence, scarcely had Bradford compiled his record of
prisoners on hand than he was opening negotiations
with the enemy in New York, aiming at the release of
some of the unfortunates languishing in the British
prison ships in Wallabout Bay.[6]

The Navy Board's inspection of the *Saratoga*
spelled the end of Francis Lewis' hopes of getting her
off promptly on another cruise. Between the storm
of October 7 and the *Elizabeth*'s guns enough damage had been done to the sloop-of-war to necessitate a
rather thorough overhauling. One ball had smashed
most of the coaming around a hatch. Several others
had crashed through her stout pine sheathing, while
innumerable chocks either had been shot away in the
encounter or carried away during the gale. Added to
that was the need of doing a better job of fishing the
bowsprit than the makeshift repairs at sea and of re-
placing considerable studding. Young agreed with
the carpenters. He sent word regretfully to Lewis
that it would be imperative to bring the *Saratoga* up
to Philadelphia and put her in the Continental shipyard. She required the expert attention of Joshua
Humphreys. There were various minor delays after
that, and October had almost ended before the sloop-
of-war came through the chevaux-de-frise and was
turned over to the care of the master builder.[7]

Long before that John Young had become famous.
One has but to read the newspapers of the Revolutionary War period to realize that it took a deed of
magnificent proportions to evoke an adjective from
an editorial pen. Journalism was staid, perfunctory,
unimaginative, and prosaic. It dealt in matter-of-fact
rhetoric. But it was generally accurate. In that October of 1780, the captain shook the Philadelphia editors
out of their calm. The *Pennsylvania Packet* gave unusual space to the cruise of the *Saratoga* "commanded
by the gallant Captain John Young." It described
the taking of the *Elizabeth* and the *Nancy* "in which
as well as in the former action [with the *Charming
Molly*] the greatest bravery and good conduct was
displayed by the worthy commander of the Saratoga."
It spoke of the other captures as adding to "this well-
merited success of Captain Young."[8] The editor of
the *Pennsylvania Gazette,* published a day later, could
think of no greater eulogy and reprinted the entire
masterpiece.[9]

To John Young these tributes must have sounded
sweet indeed after the lean years since the spring of
1778. Only once before had the newspapers given his
goings and comings more than a passing paragraph,
and that had been not of his own accomplishments but
of his news from Europe as he had learned it at Martinique upon his second voyage in the *Independence*.[10]
But now he was "the gallant Captain John Young"—
the toast of the town—and why not? Never since the
earlier days of the war had the port of Philadelphia
witnessed the return of a Continental ship from so
glorious a cruise. For many a long month, the patient
Whig populace had been starving for a naval hero.

They had one now—a man who had stood a double test—a hero to the public and to his own crew as well. It was not just the newspapers who called him gallant, and brave, and worthy. One of his officers, speaking for himself and his companions, lauded the captain, too, as "venturesome and full of ardour"—the beau ideal of a dashing commander.[11]

Even the account that had come via New York soon after his return of the capture at sea of Henry Laurens could not throw a damper upon the captain's exuberance. Looking back upon the first cruise in the *Saratoga,* the climax seemed a logical one to the captain; an unfortunate end to the serio-comic convoy of the packet *Mercury.* Perhaps he gave it no other thought just then, for the day before, the prize *Two Brothers* had come up the Delaware, and he was busy preparing the necessary libel against her.[12]

As more days passed, John Young grew anxious about the rest of his prizes, particularly those three richly ladened Jamaicamen. He had no hopes for the *Providence,* but had the other three shared her fate and fallen again into British hands? They were long overdue. Would the sloop *Elizabeth* and the sloop *Two Brothers* be the only prizes of all six to reach port? By the end of October, fears had become a certainty, and it needed only the first week in November for dispatches from New York to bring confirmation. There would be no twenty thousand pounds prize money in Continental or any other kind of currency for Midshipman Livingston; nor for anyone else. The *Charming Molly,* the *Elizabeth,* and the *Nancy* had all been retaken.[13]

Admiral George Brydges Rodney's squadron of ships of the line and frigates had robbed John Young of the finest fruits of his spectacular cruise. First of the prizes to be retaken had been the brig *Providence.* Midshipman Penfield made a gallant effort to escape, but the mighty spread of canvas on the *Alcide* was too much for him. The master's log of the giant seventy-four carried a laconic note for the morning of October 11: "½ past 10 Came up with the Chace found her to be a Brigg from Jamica Bound to New York. Just before Taken by an American privateer. Sent people on board the prize."

The prize crew carried the *Providence* into New York, where, when Captain Walter Young of the *Alcide* libeled against her, the captains of the frigates *Triton* and *Guadaloupe* filed an answer, claiming earlier capture and praying "that the prize may be judged lawfully the property of the officers and crews" of those two frigates. Depositions were taken in the Admiralty Court before Judge Robert Bayard. The former mate of the *Providence,* who had been left on board when she originally had been taken, testified that "the last voyage of the Providence was from Philadelphia to Port au Prince with lumber. On her return voyage to Philadelphia with sugar and coffee she was seized by H.M.S. Guadaloupe and Triton. She was manned by those ships and ordered to New York. She was afterwards taken by the Saratoga, who sent Nathaniel Pinfield on board as Prize Master to take her to Philadelphia, but she was captured by H.M.S. Alcide." As the "said Brigantine having been then a few hours in the possession of the rebels," the court awarded the *Providence* to the *Alcide*.[14]

Three hours after the *Providence* had been taken on the morning of October 11, and many leagues farther south, two more of Rodney's ships, the *Intrepid,* of sixty-four guns, and the frigate *Raleigh,* espied the *Charming Molly* limping toward the Virginia capes and set out in pursuit. Barney had no chance to elude them. He fled as best he could during a three-hour period from one o'clock to four o'clock in the afternoon, when the *Raleigh* came abreast. The Stars and Stripes were lowered as the *Raleigh* "at 4 brought too Chace. found her a Ship from the West Indies bound to New York, but taken by a Rebel Privateer. took out the Prisoners and the Intrepid mann'd her."[15]

The *Saratoga*'s lieutenant and his eight men were then transferred to the *Intrepid,*[16] where Barney faced her captain, the Honorable Anthony James Pye Molloy and discovered himself in the hands of "the greatest tyrant in the British Navy." The Lieutenant's treatment on board the *Intrepid* during the balance of the cruise seems to warrant this stigmatization. Years afterwards his daughter-in-law took from Barney's own lips an account of this experience. During the passage to New York, she reported, he was kept *on the poop,* with no shelter from the weather; in this situation he was exposed to the severity of a cold snow storm of several days continuance, *without clothes or bedding."* The italics are those of the daughter-in-law, who does not, however, explain the phenomenon of a two-day snowstorm on the Atlantic in mid-October.[17]

How, when, and by whom the *Nancy* was retaken has not been recorded. All we know is that Sailing Master Garvin was no more fortunate than Barney and Penfield in eluding the British cordon and that on October 23 the brig arrived in New York, sent in by one of His Majesty's ships.[18]

The *Elizabeth,* the biggest and best of Young's prizes, owed her recapture not so much to the vigilance of the enemy as to friction between Prizemaster Faggo and his second in command, John Hackett. The latter told the story months later with painstaking detail, "lest there should any blame be laid on me by Captain Young." In his lengthy narrative, he never mentioned Faggo by name. He called him "a youngster," commenting that "I believe Captain Young was not Acquainted with the gentlemans Abilities or he would not have sent him Over me."

When the *Elizabeth* parted with the *Saratoga,* according to Hackett, an observation was taken which placed the ship in 38.16° north latitude, and about thirty miles from the coast. That night they got in shore and with the wind out of the north, made short stretches off and on. "Our commander never had a thought of bending cables, or any other preparation necessary to be made when you make the Land," was Hackett's sour comment. At dawn an enemy frigate was sighted and gave chase to them. The wind had veered easterly so it was possible to run northward along the coast with the intention, should they be overhauled, of beaching the ship rather than of being taken. By afternoon pursuit ended, and Faggo, as

Hackett averred, wanted to put about claiming he could not depend upon his observations and felt they were far north of the Delaware capes.

"I sayed not," Hackett recorded, "but he would put the ship About and Stand to the Southw.ᵈ" Hackett was convinced that if the course had been continued northerly they would have made the Cape Henlopen lighthouse in two or three hours, and, as the wind continued easterly for thirty-six hours, they by that time could have reached Philadelphia. As the weather was thick, Faggo did agree to come to anchor until it cleared. Next morning Hackett requested permission to take the boat and go ashore, being sure they were off Sinepuxent, Maryland, and wishing to convince his superior that they were headed in the wrong direction. The colloquy, as Hackett recorded it was amusing: "he [Faggo] answered he would not spare me out of the ship and that it was dangerous to Send the Boat and people out of the Ship for fear of loosing her and them on the Beach I told him I would Swim from the Boat to the shore and let her lay off for me untill I came back, on which he Say'd he would not take Charge of the ship If I left her I offered to take charge of the ship If he would go ashore but All would not do he must heave up and Stand further Southerly."

Another observation indicated they were south of the Delaware capes, but again the prizemaster would not believe it. The land visible a few miles distant looked to him like the New Jersey coast near Egg Harbor, and the soundings agreed with those indicated for that area upon a chart of ancient vintage

which he had with him. So southward they proceeded
cautiously and the following morning made out a
great bluff point.

"I say'd there was no Such land between Sandy
Hook and Cape May," wrote Hackett, "and then requested of him what he meant to do with the ship as
I was fairly tired out of my life and patience there
being only the Boatswain that was taken in the Ship
and myself that knew what to do with her."

Faggo this time agreed to send a boat ashore for a
pilot, and Hackett took her through the shoal water
to land near Chincoteague, Virginia, some sixty miles
south of Cape Henlopen. He returned with a pilot
and confirmation of how wrong their course had been.
By then the wind was coming out of the northeast,
forcing them to beat along shore for half the distance
to the Delaware capes. When it shifted to north-
northeast, they were too short-handed to carry reefed-
topsails and "were horsed Away to Leward as far as
where we took the Pilot from."

Because of a strong southerly current, the pilot
dared not venture around the ship shoals to find a safe
anchorage, so they again headed seaward. Hackett
reported the climax briefly: "next morning we made
a Sail to windward of us which bore down upon us and
cut us off the land She being About two miles from us
and we about 9 miles of the land She proved to be the
Swift sloop of war Capt[n] Applin from N York who
took us."

In consequence, Hackett commented that when he
saw "the Gentleman's [Faggo's] weakness in the Discharge of his Duty, he was surpprized at the Capt[ns]

conduct which now makes me a prisoner." Also, he was satisfied that the commander of the *Saratoga* owed "his loss as well as mine" to the incapacity of the prizemaster.[19] It would be interesting to have Faggo's version of the same period, but there is no record of it. However, we do have confirmation of Hackett's story of the recapture in the log of His Majesty's brig *Swift,* Peter Aplin, commander, for October 19:

"At 5 [A.M.] saw a sail in the S W quarter," Captain Aplin recorded; "gave chace and cleared Ship for action At 7 she hoisted Rebel Colours, which at 8 she struck and proved to be the Ship Elizabeth, Prize to the Saratoga, a Continental Sloop of War."[20]

Faggo, Hackett, Clarkson, and their thirty-nine hands were taken on board the *Swift,*[21] and the fourth of John Young's prizes was in the hands of the enemy.

Meanwhile at New York, Rodney exulted in the success of his measures. In the same period that Young's prizes were recaptured, His Majesty's war vessels had bagged thirteen American privateers and, as the Admiral proclaimed, obliged all others "to take shelter in their Ports."[22] Four hundred prisoners had been added by these captures, which brought the total of unfortunates in British hands to 1,200 and overtaxed the capacity of the two prison ships in Wallabout Bay.[23]

This great influx of captive seamen introduced a sinister name into history—the prison ship *Jersey.* Much misinformation has been printed regarding the "Old Jersey." The popular misconception is that she flourished in all her horror from 1777 to 1783, but that is untrue. Until the advent of Rodney, in the fall of 1780, the *Jersey* had been a hospital ship, a vessel of mercy for the tars of His Majesty's navy; but, as Rodney himself reported in a letter to the Lords of the Admiralty, "The great increase of Prisoners and the extreme bad Conditions of the Prison Ships rendered it necessary to convert the Jersey Hospital Ship into a Prison Ship."[24]

Most of the enlisted men from the *Saratoga's* four prize crews found their way eventually into the dismal hulk.[25] Except in a few instances, the omnipotent Rodney refused to exchange them. Railing against "the Wretches" and "their Acts of Piracy," he turned a deaf ear to the proposals from Philadelphia. He was fully persuaded "that if their Prisoners are not released, it will be of the greatest advantage to the Commerce of His Majesty's Loyal Subjects," as well as the severest blow that could be dealt the rebels, "whose chief support arrises from the Piratical Captors they make."[26]

For seventy-one American commissioned officers—Continental and privateer—Rodney reserved a different fate. Among them were Barney, Garvin, Faggo, and Hackett. He loaded them into the lower hold of the sixty-four gun ship *Yarmouth*.[27] On November 16, he and his squadron sailed for the West Indies, and the same day the *Yarmouth* cleared for England.[28] Her captain, Skeffingham Lutwidge, had positive orders "to proceed without a moments loss of time when the Wind and Weather permits to the Downs."

On his arrival there, or at any port in England, Rodney directed him to "deliver the American Prison-

ers into the hands of the proper Agents, acquainting
him that they are Notorious Offenders without Faith
or Honor, and the necessity of keeping them Con-
fin'd, they being the Officers employ'd in the Rebel
Privateers thro' whose Means the Americans have
been enabled to continue in Rebellion."[29]

The *Yarmouth* made Plymouth on December 16—
a passage of thirty days. Hard gales had increased the
leaks which had developed even before she left New
York, and Captain Lutwidge had "found it necessary
to employ the Prisoners at the pumps, and on that
account to order them whole allowance of provisions,
the Ship's Company, from their weak & Sickly state,
being unequal to that duty."[30] This statement is certainly a contradiction of Barney's claim that during
the passage "the water was measured out to them with
even more parsimony than the food, and so thick with
animalcules was it, that they could only drink it
through their closed teeth." Moreover, Barney declared that eleven of their number perished of fever
and the survivors, "pale, emaciated feeble," were
ordered on deck at Plymouth, all "suffering from a
loathsome phthiriasis."[31] Nor does it agree with the
account given by Master's Mate Faggo to his mother
in Boston. "The 9th of November," he wrote her, "71
of us, all officers, were put on board the Yarmouth,
a 64 gun ship, in the casks of her lower hold, in about
20 foot square, only one or two allowed to come up
at a time till we were half passage over, when we were
allowed as many as could get up. But our being confined in so close and small a compass, caused a fever
among us so severe that 50 out of 71 were sick at a

time, not one of us has escaped; 6 died before our arrival."[32]

The prisoners, after a period of a month in a guard ship in Plymouth Road, during which they regained enough health and strength "to walk without leaning on each other," were formally committed to Mill Prison.[33] Three of the *Saratoga*'s officers arrived at the prison on January 9, 1781, and the fourth, Joshua Barney, a week later.[34]

CHAPTER IX

£500,000 *Security*

IF the enviable record achieved by John Young in the *Saratoga* was a topic upon which Francis Lewis waxed eloquent, he had a basis for his enthusiasm. Had he not, as a member of the Marine Committee back in 1776, sponsored Young for a captaincy in the Continental navy? And had he not, earlier in the present year, appointed Young to the new sloop-of-war despite the doubts of those who could recall only that captain's misfortune in losing the brigantine *Independence* by shipwreck? The dashing October cruise had rewarded the faith of the Chairman of the Board of Admiralty beyond fondest hopes and had afforded opportunity for modest crowing.

No one could begrudge Lewis his elation, for aside from the *Saratoga*'s success, the Board of Admiralty had little else to brag about. To it had been assigned the hopeless task of waging naval warfare with an empty treasury, an exhausted credit, and a demoralized currency. Its heritage was four years of well-meaning but inefficient committee operation in competition with the alluring and profitable trade of privateering—four years, during which ship after ship had been lost and the seafaring population alienated from a service promising little but misery, privation, and perhaps death or captivity. Add to this, a Board of Admiralty seldom able to command a quorum, an authority subject to Congressional whims, and among certain captains a spirit of independence bordering upon insubordination—and one marvels that the creaking machinery functioned at all.

No doubt Francis Lewis wondered, too, as in early November, he presented the woeful picture to Congress, with an earnest request "that some mode may be adopted for the present that will accelerate the equipment of their Navy." Four Continental ships-of-war were fitting out in the Delaware, he pointed out, and almost hourly requests were received for them, generally of a nature requiring immediate action. As the Board of Admiralty consisted of but three members (although Congress had decreed a five-man membership with three constituting a quorum), "no one member will presume to Issue orders in the absence of the others." Therefore, with two members in constant attendance upon Congress, Lewis protested that "the service is often impeded or delayed."[1] Yet nothing came of this and a subsequent appeal save replacement of the two Congressional members by two others, who could spare no more time to naval matters than their predecessors.[2]

Lack of money, however, was causing greater delay than lack of quorum. Of Congress' magnificent gesture of $700,000 the previous August, there remained unpaid $426,747, "without which," as Lewis patiently explained, "it will be impossible to get the Confederacy and Saratoga equipped," or the *Deane* provisioned for a cruise.[3] The Board had just received Joshua Humphreys' bill for repairs to the *Saratoga*.

Much material had been used—202 pounds of oakum, 160 feet of scantling, 296 feet of various size pine boards and planks, and 40 chocks. Then there had been a wharfage charge, another for superintending the work, and 86 days of labor, making a grand total cost of £73.2.9.[4] Reduced to Continental currency, the amount was more than $25,000.00.

The Continental share of Young's first prize, the *Sarah,* sold at the Coffee House late in September, had been applied toward repairing the *Confederacy.*[5] The two prizes reaching port from the October cruise —the sloops *Elizabeth* and *Two Brothers*—were undergoing condemnation, but no sales had yet been made.[6] No wonder Francis Lewis was calling upon Congress for the unpaid balance due the Board. He had stopped work on the ship of the line building at Portsmouth and was ready to recommend her sale to France.[7] Connecticut had failed to come to his aid financially, and the frigate at Middletown was little nearer completion than she had been two months earlier.[8] To cap all these misfortunes, the *Confederacy,* which seemed to be the unluckiest ship afloat, had her head carried away in a river collision off Penrose's wharf, the accident happening just as Lewis was figuring her as once more ready for sea. A newly launched letter-of-marque ship, the *Shelaly,* had been caught by a flood tide and carried afoul the Continental frigate.[9]

Coincident with the financial stringency was a near mutiny on board the *Trumbull* in the river below Philadelphia. This frigate and the *Deane* had been lying off Chester ever since the return from their profitless foray along the Atlantic coast. Both crews originally had shipped at Boston for a single cruise.[10] While the men in the *Deane* were willing to remain longer in service, the doughty mariners in the *Trumbull* were not. Their time was up on November 6, and they wanted their pay and liberty to depart. James Nicholson, who tried hard to prevail upon them to continue for a short cruise, or at least sail the frigate around to Boston, knew what was at the bottom of the trouble. Petty officers and two-thirds of the crew already had agreed to sign on board several privately owned vessels outfitting in the Delaware. It was the old story of the lure of privateering versus the underpaid Continental service. To none of Nicholson's reasons would they listen. For a few minutes it looked as if the entire crew would leave the ship, discharge or no discharge, pay or no pay. Finally, a compromise was reached. They would remain on board long enough to take the frigate up to Philadelphia, but if they were not properly released then, there would be trouble. To prevent the same spirit infecting the men on board the *Deane,* Nicholson ordered his brother to drop down to Reedy Island.[11]

Several weeks earlier, sensing the inevitable disintegration of his crew, James Nicholson had cast an envious glance at the *Confederacy,* a larger and better frigate. He could marshal several reasons why he should command her. Was he not senior captain in the navy? Would it be well, were the vessels acting in concert, that a junior in rank should command the larger ship? Had not his services entitled him to favorable consideration? So he memorialized Congress for the appointment, and Congress referred it to the Board of Admiralty.[12] On November 13 Francis Lewis urged Congress to accede to the memorial, advancing not only the right of seniority, but an additional, odd reason: under Nicholson the *Confederacy* might be manned immediately, "which is of great importance at this autumn season before the navigation of the river is obstructed by ice."[13] How a captain who could not induce his own crew to remain would be able to conjure up a crew for the *Confederacy* was not explained. Congress ignored the recommendation, and the eldest Nicholson brother decided that the *Trumbull,* even with a vanishing crew, was better than no command at all. He brought her up to Philadelphia in mid-November,[14] and two-thirds of his complement departed—many properly discharged, the rest over the side after dark. Congress, thereupon, authorized the Board of Admiralty to send the frigate on a six-month cruise, for the protection of the trade but did not specify where or how the money could be secured to recruit a crew for that purpose.[15]

Only the *Deane* was ready for sea, and Congress already had taken over her direction along with a curt inquiry of the Board of Admiralty as to why public clothing and military stores down in Hispaniola had not been brought to the Continent. Congress proposed sending the *Deane* down to Carabasse, at Cap François without delay. Would Mr. Lewis please see that this was done, ordering the frigate first to Maryland for sufficient tobacco to pay for the charges that had accrued against the long-held Beaumarchais stores?[16] Samuel Nicholson had no desire, apparently, to go to the West Indies at that time. Business matters, he explained, necessitated his presence in Boston. Leave of absence was given him and a successor was appointed ad interim. The successor was the youngest of the Nicholson brothers, John.[17]

By November 20, the *Deane* had sailed, and with her vanished Lewis' last hope for that cherished joint cruise in force. One vessel upon which he had banked was unfinished on the ways; the *Alliance,* still at Boston, was the seat of a court martial likely to engage her officers indefinitely;[18] the *Trumbull* had no crew in prospect. There remained only the *Confederacy* and the *Saratoga;* upon these two the Board of Admiralty lavished full attention.

During November, John Young had been applying himself assiduously to the multitudinous duties involved in getting his vessel refitted. This business occupied his days, and in the evenings, he, his wife, and William Semple forgathered around the fireplace in the cozy Laurel street home. There, with the little Negro Favorite to keep the toddy hot and the glasses filled, they discussed many matters, the most important of which was investment of his private funds. Semple had about made up his mind to embark in foreign trade, and wanted Young in partnership. They worked out the details during those pleasant sessions. The outcome was an agreement that the Youngs would join with the Philadelphia merchant in acquiring a ship and a small brig, Semple financing the major portion. From this partnership in the next year came the ship *Dove,* of which the Youngs owned one-sixteenth, and the brigantine *Joanna,* in which they had a one-eighth interest.[19]

Most important of Young's official duties was to replace the officers who had been taken in his four prizes. He had been hopeful for their liberation, for

Barney's in particular, and as late as November 17, through Deputy Commissary of Prisoners Thomas Bradford, was proposing the exchange of Captain Robert Gill of the *Charming Molly* for the *Saratoga*'s first lieutenant.[20] This failing, Blaney Allison was promoted from second to first lieutenant,[21] and the vacancy thus created was filled by the appointment of James Pyne as second lieutenant.[22]

This officer was an ideal selection. He was a veteran of the South Carolina navy, which he had entered in 1776 as a second lieutenant, advancing to a captaincy the next year.[23] As commander of the brig *Comet,* he had been captured early in 1778 by His Majesty's frigate *Daphne,*[24] and had been for some time a prisoner in New York.[25] Upon his return to Charleston, he had been appointed commander of the brig *Hornet,*[26] and by a singular coincidence, he had fallen afoul of the same British frigate in April, 1779. This time, while he lost his brig, Pyne escaped to shore in a longboat.[27] His next command, the galley *Rutledge,* had been destroyed by the British during the Savannah campaign of the same year.[28] His last service had been as commander of a former French ship, the *Truite,* armed with twenty-six 12-pounders.[29] In the futile defense of Charleston, the *Truite* had been sunk as part of a barrier in the Cooper River.[30] Sent with the rest of the naval officers to Philadelphia on parole, he had been exchanged, and, with his first lieutenant on July 18, made a tender of service to Congress. There was nothing they more ardently wished, they said, "than an opportunity to signalize ourselves in any service in the Naval Department that Your Honors may think proper to point out."[31] "Their

Honors" referred the memorial to the Board of Admiralty, which had no openings until October.[32] By then Pyne's lieutenant had gone into private service, but the captain was still at hand. Lewis recommended him on October 25, as worthy "the Rank of a Lieutenant in the navy of the United States," and he was forthwith appointed to the *Saratoga*.[33]

The record is blank as to the sailing master who replaced John Garvin, but Joseph Bailey was shipped as a master's mate, succeeding either Faggo or Hackett.[34] One midshipman, Nathaniel Penfield, was exchanged for Midshipman Thackstone, who had been taken in the *Providence*. Penfield rejoined the *Saratoga* in November.[35] There was a change of marine officers also. Abraham Van Dyke resigned, probably because of advanced age and too strenuous a life on the sloop-of-war, and his place was filled by Lieutenant Hugh Kirkpatrick. All that is known of the new lieutenant of marines is that on December 11, 1780, he issued a power of attorney to William Geddis, a citizen of Philadelphia.[36]

Only one defection is recorded among the *Saratoga*'s hands. Anthony Castoff, a Negro, deserted on November 25. In advertising for his return, Young described him as "a shoemaker by trade, but has been to sea sometime, and will pass for a seaman, about five feet ten inches high, black complexion, talks French, Spanish, and tolerable good English . . . Had on, when he went away, a brown outside jacket with horn buttons, a lincey under jacket, and long canvas trousers."[37] The description also provides a fair picture of the uniform of a seaman in the Continental navy.

The *Saratoga,* despite this one elopement, was the

most popular ship in the navy. Young's success in her
had made recruiting comparatively easy, and all gaps
in the complement were filled promptly.

After mid-November, when the sloop-of-war was
released finally from the Continental shipyard, Young
gave her his undivided attention. She rode at anchor
in the stream off the city until such time as the Navy
Board could provide provisions and ammunition. As
the Navy Board, in turn, had to await money from the
Board of Admiralty, there was delay until the Continental shares of the captain's prizes were available.
The sloop *Elizabeth* had been sold by public auction
at the Coffee House on November 9, and the *Two
Brothers* went under the hammer about ten days
later.[38] By frugal application, the money would prove
sufficient to take care of the needs of both the *Saratoga*
and the *Confederacy.*

As November drew to a close, the *Confederacy,*
after lying "at Philadª and Chester—Careening,
Rigging, Manning, &c. being near seven months,"
was at least ready to sail.[39] To help round out her complement, the Pennsylvania Supreme Executive Council consigned a number of felons to her, pardoning
them upon the condition that they serve for the dura-
tion of the war.[40] Captain Harding, meanwhile, had
decided to help himself and while off Chester resorted
to a practice which had gotten him into hot water a
year before. Vessel after vessel was boarded, and
likely seamen impressed. One week of this and a
mighty howl arose from the Supreme Executive
Council. It had been lenient the year before, being
unwilling to interrupt important Congressional business, but the limit had been reached. The "abuses of

our Trade, Oppression of our Citizens & other Ir-
regularities of Capt. Harding & his Officers" would
have to be stopped.[41] Congress referred the protest
to a committee of three, one of whom was a member of
the Board of Admiralty.[42] Procrastination ensued—
enough to let Harding drop down the river below the
Pennsylvania boundary—after which the protest was
referred to the Board of Admiralty "to take orders
thereon."[43] That concluded the matter, although on
the same day, off Newcastle, Delaware, and safely
out of the jurisdiction of Pennsylvania, Harding "Impressed seven Men out of a Schooner from Sea."[44]

With the *Confederacy* gone below, the task of
policing the river for deserters fell to John Young.
There were plenty of them skulking about, hiding
in small craft or dodging around the wharves, all bent
upon getting on board privateers. A number had
skipped from the *Confederacy*,[45] as well as those previously reported from the *Trumbull*. As senior captain
in the navy, James Nicholson had ordered Young "to
take up and secure" any he found.[46] Supplementing
this verbal order, on December 4, Francis Lewis had
instructed Young to assist the Deputy Commissary
of Prisoners in seizing any escaped prisoners or deserters found on board any vessels in the river.[47]

Under these orders, Young conceived himself justified "in entering on board any private armed or merchant vessel in this harbour either sailing out or into
port and examin[ing] their papers as well as to
observe whether they may have contraband goods on
board." And on December 7, in line with this con-
ception of his duty, he hailed a small shallop passing
by on the way down river. As the shallop stopped

there was a furtive scurrying about the deck. On board went the captain to find five seamen hiding in the cabin. A little questioning disclosed that all five were deserters from the *Trumbull*. Back to the *Saratoga* he herded them, and then forgot the incident.[48]

Had Seth Harding's conduct in impressing seamen not been under fire at that time, probably everybody else would have forgotten the case of the *Trumbull*'s deserters, or would not have had the temerity to protest. But Pennsylvania was officially in arms against impressments, and the five deserters on the shallop had engaged to enter various letter-of-marque vessels, owned by a group of prominent Philadelphia merchants, which were lying in the stream off Chester. The deserters were, in fact, on their way down to join their respective vessels when Young seized them. Blair McClenachan, owner of the privateer *Fair American;* Francis Gurney & Co., owners of the *Morning Star;* Bunner, Murray & Co., owners of the *Charming Sally;* and Thomas Leaming, Jr., and Joshua Fisher, owners of the *Comet,* put their heads together, and resorted to legal action.[49]

William Will, high sheriff of Philadelphia county, boarded the *Saratoga* on the morning of December 9, armed with a plea of trespass signed by the letter-of-marque ships' owners. Young met him at the rail, heard the formal document read, and refused to surrender the five deserters. There were arguments, threats, and recriminations. The captain's temper flared, even as it had flared under provocation in the past. The high sheriff retaliated by announcing sonorously that he was placing Captain John Young, of the Continental sloop-of-war *Saratoga,* under arrest, that he would return to shore and issue a writ of habeas corpus to remove the five men, and that he would insist that the court fix a security of £500,000 against this highhanded Continental officer who presumed to flout and resist an officer of the law.

Staggered by the injustice of the proceedings, Young landed shortly afterwards and hastened to the Board of Admiralty office. To Francis Lewis he described what had happened and demanded Congressional protection.

"Five hundred thousand pounds security is excessive and unreasonable," he declared. "If such a sum is fixed, I have no alternative but to go to jail, which is cruel treatment for doing what I conceive to be my duty." [50]

To term £500,000 bail merely "excessive and unreasonable" was putting it mildly. It amounted to about two and one-half million Continental dollars. Since on November 22 it had been decreed that Continental money compared with specie be fixed at seventy-five for one, [51] Young's bail in hard dollars would amount to approximately $33,300.00.

Francis Lewis took up the cudgels for his protégé. It was high time, if the Continental service was to survive, to call for a showdown. Young's detailed report of the occurrence was presented to Congress that afternoon.

"The Board on the foregoing state of facts beg leave to report as their opinion that Captain Young ought to be supported by Congress against such litigious suits" it declared; "and that he may not be thereby delayed from executing the orders of this Board which he has received for proceeding im-

mediately to sea to cruize against the Common
Enemy."[52]

Congress took no action; at least the journal is
mute on the subject. From subsequent developments,
it appears that secret counsel was given Lewis to get
Young out on a cruise at once and keep him away
from Philadelphia for a few months. What happened
to the five deserters from the *Trumbull* is not divulged.

During the next five days the Navy Board met all
requisitions for provisions, slops, and ammunition.
Then on December 15, the captain received his sailing
orders, those Lewis claimed to have handed him previously having been but a subterfuge. Gathering in
the lower Delaware was a fleet of merchantmen bound
for Hispaniola. To these he was to give a short convoy
off the coast.[53] Perhaps he might meet the *Confederacy* in the lower bay. If so, he and Harding could
act in concert. Destination of both was Cap François,
where by early spring a merchant fleet would be laden
and ready to return. In the West Indies they would
find the *Deane*. She, with the *Confederacy* and the
Saratoga, should convoy the merchantmen back to
the Continent. Whatever of the Beaumarchais stores
in the hands of M. Carabasse that could not be placed
in the *Deane* should be divided between the *Confederacy* and the *Saratoga*.[54] Also, there was the usual
injunction to look for the second division of the French
fleet—a division which, it turned out, never did arrive.[55]

On the sloop-of-war all was ready for unobtrusive
departure. Francis Lewis wished Young a successful
voyage and left for the Board of Admiralty office.
Mistress Young bade her captain farewell in the

quietude of his cabin. She it was who set down for us the date when her husband put out on his final cruise. She gave no details of their parting; she did not dream it was the final good-by. Many times before she had seen him sail away, and always he had returned. So when they put her ashore, and she watched the canvas fill in the sharp December wind as the *Saratoga* got under way, she could have no premonition that he would never come back.[56]

Thus he vanished from the sight of the friends who wished him well and those privateer owners who had put a price upon his head for doing his duty.

CHAPTER X

The Sea-Fighter Sails South

THE winter cruise of the *Saratoga* began in discomfort. That December of 1780 was a nasty one, with chill in the air and dense blankets of fog hanging over the Delaware to obscure shore line and river buoys. Delays were inevitable in negotiating the twisting channel through the chevaux-de-frise below the city and again opposite Billingsport. Time was lost, too, in exchanging pilots at Chester so that not until the morning of December 18 did the sloop-of-war drop anchor off Reedy Island, the rendezvous for the merchant fleet. The gray pall still clung to the surface of the water, but through it was discernible the tall sides of the thirty-six gun frigate *Confederacy*. Harding had not yet sailed.[1]

During the three-day passage downstream, John Young had completed quartering his men. There were many new faces among the hands to replace the sixty-odd unfortunates who had terminated their naval careers in the New York prison ships. But of the tried and proved veterans of the October cruise some seventy stalwarts remained, and the newcomers were distributed among them so that each watch had a good proportion of the original crew. Gun crews were handled in the same fashion. Leaving in the capable hands of Lieutenant Allison the routine of distributing slops, drawing up returns, and arranging the messes, the captain rowed over in the late afternoon to the *Confederacy.*

The situation might have been embarrassing. Young's commission antedated Harding's by several years.[2] Thus there existed the anomaly of the senior officer commanding an eighteen gun sloop-of-war, and the junior officer a large frigate. The very possibility of such a contingency had sent James Nicholson seeking a larger command a month or more before. There could have been unpleasantness here, but Young was tactful. He merely informed Harding that as their destinations were identical, he proposed joining the *Confederacy* in the cruise. He asked also if the whole merchant fleet had assembled and if the frigate was ready to sail.[3]

Only the weather was now detaining him, Harding explained. He had about 260 men on board—26 by impressments since leaving Philadelphia. He would have had more, he added, were he "invested with power similar to the British Navy in such Cases." No doubt he told Young how one resolute privateersman, a few days before, had called his bluff when he tried his favorite tactics.[4] At any rate, his complement would suffice. As to the merchantmen, there were thirteen of them anchored somewhere around in the fog, all bound for Hispaniola, Cuba, or the Dutch Islands.[5]

Signals were agreed upon, and Young returned to the *Saratoga.* There he busied himself with the merchant captains, arranging the details of the convoy and promising them a good offing. Most of them carried valuable cargoes of flour and tobacco for Cap François, Havana, and St. Eustatius.[6]

Propitious weather for departure came with dawn of December 20. Young flung out the signal to make sail, and the fleet got under way. They ran down into Delaware Bay about two leagues; then the wind failed. At ten o'clock, however, a fresh breeze sprang up from the northwest, and the voyage was resumed. Abreast of Bombay Hook the day grew squally. It made no difference to Young, but Harding's pilot, who also feared the nearly spent tide, was dismayed. Consequently, the *Confederacy* came to anchor, and the convoying job devolved entirely upon the *Saratoga*. At Lewes, Delaware, the "all clear" flag was flying from the lighthouse, and just before dusk Young took the sloop-of-war and the thirteen merchantmen out to sea. Once again, Francis Lewis' hopes of a joint cruise—even a modified one—had been dashed.[7]

Well southeast of Cape Henlopen on the next afternoon, a merchantman far out on the port of the fleet signaled presence of a strange sail. A string of pennants rising to the spanker gaff of the *Saratoga*, ordered the vessels to proceed upon their course, and John Young, scenting action, veered from his position in the van of the convoy. An hour later, he was in full chase of a small ship—a privateer without a doubt— which had abandoned all thoughts of cutting a merchantman out of the American fleet at first sight of the trim sloop-of-war.[8]

Few were the vessels afloat which could outsail the *Saratoga* now that she was properly ballasted, and the British privateer *Resolution,* fresh out of New York,

was not numbered among them. Within another hour
Young was within gunshot. A warning ball from a
4-pounder was disregarded by the Britisher. Then,
as an engagement seemed inevitable, Captain John
Laughton of the *Resolution* tacked to bring his broadside to bear upon the onrushing pursuer. Young
tacked too at just the proper moment, and both ships
fired simultaneously. The privateer's fire was high,
cutting a few shrouds and putting several large shot
holes in the billowing sails on the sloop-of-war. But
the *Saratoga*'s 9-pounders, served even as they had
been the previous October, sent an iron hail into the
hull and across the deck of their opponent. It was all
over in a few minutes. Laughton had no taste for
further punishment. His flag came down on the run.[9]

John Young took possession at once. The *Resolution* was full ship-rigged, of 100 tons burden, and
mounted sixteen 6-pounder carriage guns.[10] She had
a crew of better than fifty men and during the preceding autumn had been fairly successful in her cruises
along the Atlantic coast.[11] Unfortunately for her, in
inaugurating her winter cruise she had picked on the
wrong convoy.

Transfer of the captured Britons to the *Saratoga*
presented a problem. The captain did not want to be
burdened with so many prisoners on a long voyage.
To land them meant abandoning the merchantmen.
Inasmuch as the convoy was already hull down to the
southwest, it was a question whether they could be
overtaken. Certainly, he could not pick them up before dark, and there was every possibility of missing
them in the night. His decision, finally, was to put
about and make for Cape Henlopen, letting the fleet

shift for itself. As a result, several days later, five of them were captured and sent into New York, giving the enemy its first news of the large convoy which had sailed from Philadelphia.[12]

Reaching Cape Henlopen was not so easy as it sounded. Winds were contrary, and it took the *Saratoga* full ten days to beat back to the Delaware. On New Year's Day, 1781, the captain hove to off the lighthouse, and sent a boat ashore with a letter asking Henry Fisher to provide a militia guard. During the period at sea, he had cajoled a number of the privateer's crew into signing up in the *Saratoga*. Eighteen remained obdurate to his blandishments, and these eighteen he landed at Lewes. Colonel Fisher accepted them and sent them northward to the custody of the Deputy Commissary of Prisoners.[13]

John Young, meanwhile, had manned the *Resolution* with a prize crew and put on board, as prisoners, the three lieutenants of the privateer.[14] Captain Laughton was kept on board the *Saratoga*. About sunset, the prize stood through the capes and up the bay. She carried Young's return list for December 20, 1780, the last muster roll of the little sloop-of-war ever to reach the Board of Admiralty.[15] The prize-master turned her over to the Continental agent in Philadelphia on January 5. She was libeled against immediately, condemned in five days, and sold at the London Coffee House, "with all her tackle, apparel and furniture," on January 18.[16] It was fast work, but the Board of Admiralty needed its share of the prize money.

Learning that the *Confederacy* had gone out on December 21—the day after he and the convoy had cleared the capes—John Young resumed his interrupted cruise that same New Year's Day that he had come into Lewes.[17] Nine days later, well at sea and in about latitude 30° north, the captain fought his greatest battle.

Forth from St. Augustine, the capital of "His Majesty's loyal province of East Florida," the letter-of-marque ship *Tonyn* had sailed in early January. Named for the governor of the province, commanded by a gallant Britisher, Captain John R. Wade, armed with twenty long 9-pounders, and manned by a crew of about one hundred men, she was considered a match for any American vessel below the rating of a frigate and, perhaps, even good enough to beat off a Continental frigate at that. Her destination was Liverpool, England, whither she was carrying a cargo of turpentine, indigo, staves, hides, and deerskins—all items much prized in the mother country.[18]

This was the ship which a lookout on the *Saratoga* picked out to the southward on the bright, sunshiny morning of Tuesday, January 9. They were clear of the northern winter by then, enjoying the soft zephyrs warmed by the nearby Gulf Stream, and standing along with all canvas set. There was no need to change position; their course was carrying them directly down upon the strange sail.

Nor on the *Tonyn,* as the sloop-of-war approached, did Captain Wade see any point in avoiding the encounter. If this should turn out to be a rebel privateer, she would soon learn she had caught a tartar. So he kept his bow pointed eastward and prepared to give the enemy a reception that would surprise her. He could see he had but a small ship to deal with, and as has been said the Britisher feared only a frigate.

On the *Saratoga,* as they bowled nearer, the men exulted at the prospects. The reckless courage of their captain had imbued the entire crew with like audacity —the veterans since the days of the October cruise, the newer hands since the one crashing broadside which had silenced the privateer *Resolution.* Gunners at their stations, moveable gear stripped from the deck, powder monkeys slipping from magazine to the 9- and 4-pounders, the sloop-of-war came rushing along to the encounter, with the Stars and Stripes rippling from her top. Some five hundred yards distant, John Young ordered the helm to port, and the *Saratoga* veered until she was abreast of and running on a parallel course with the *Tonyn.* The ten gunports along the ship's port side were visible to the naked eye as the captain hailed:

"Strike your flag! This is the Continental sloop-of-war *Saratoga,* John Young commanding. What ship is that?"

Captain Wade may or may not have heard of the *Saratoga.* Her exploits in October had been rather generously reprinted in the Tory newspapers of New York and Charleston. But whether she was Continental or letter-of-marque daunted him not in the least.

"The *Tonyn,* John R. Wade, commanding," he called back. "St. Augustine to Liverpool."

And hoping to gain the advantage of surprise, in the same breath he gave the command to fire. The

British broadside screamed high through the *Saratoga*'s shrouds.[19]

Not so the response, which came like a thunderbolt from the muzzles of the *Saratoga*'s starboard battery. Nine-pound shot crashed into the ship's side, some right at the bulwarks, sending splinters hurtling through the air and wounding several men. Within a few minutes, the area was a nightmare of detonations. Both vessels fired as rapidly as guns could be loaded, run out, aimed, discharged, run in, swabbed out, reloaded, and run out again. Heavy smoke drifted aloft to be whipped away by the breeze. Through it, Young caught glimpses of his adversary and held grimly abreast of her. From all reports that came to him from the various stations, the enemy fire was causing little damage save aloft. What execution his own guns were doing, he could only surmise. He had trained his men to make each shot count, and there was precision to their fire.

What John Young surmised, Captain Wade experienced. Within a half hour several of the *Tonyn*'s 9-pounders were put out of commission, with carnage among the gun crews. The well-directed fire from the *Saratoga* was sweeping the deck. A hurtling splinter felled the British captain, wounding him badly. The first lieutenant took command. Fifteen minutes later, he too was carried below to be laid beside his superior in a cockpit filled with wounded.[20] The second lieutenant, now in command, fought on until, through the gray, pungent battle smoke, he saw the *Saratoga* looming closer, maneuvering to board. Scarcely a man remained standing on the *Tonyn*'s deck, and the bullets from the muskets of the marines on his opponent's quarter-deck were whining uncomfortably about his ears. All of his guns were silent, the crews either swept away or forced to seek shelter below. So he struck his flag. The engagement had lasted exactly one hour.[21]

How severe had been the slaughter on the *Tonyn,* the boarding officer reported a little later to Young. Seven men had been killed and fifty wounded, including most of the officers. The ship was badly torn above deck but had escaped serious damage below the water line.[22] By contrast, the *Saratoga* had not a man wounded. The sloop-of-war's sails had been sliced to ribbons, and much of her rigging had been cut; otherwise she was uninjured.[23]

For twenty-four hours, the two vessels lay side by side, while the wounded were being cared for and repairs made. Captain Wade and his injured subordinates were taken on board the *Saratoga* and put under Surgeon Brown's care. The enlisted men were made as comfortable as possible in their own cockpit. All able-bodied prisoners were transferred to the sloop-of-war. Rigging repairs were made quickly and fresh sailcloth brought up to replace the sheets that had been torn to shreds. By the time he was ready to resume his cruise, John Young had made up his mind to carry the *Tonyn* with him to Cap François. Her cargo would be more valuable in the West India market than in Philadelphia, and her damaged hull might fare badly in the winter winds off the North Atlantic coast. When they got under way on the morning of January 11, the vessels sailed southward in company.[24]

East of the Bahamas, just a week after the capture

of the *Tonyn,* the *Saratoga* took her last and richest prize of the cruise. The victim was a small, lightly armed brig, the *Douglass,* bound from Madeira to Charleston, South Carolina, with a cargo of 300 pipes of the famous product of the island from which she hailed—Madeira wine. She offered no resistance; her master, Archibald Gregg, promptly hove to when a warning shot crossed his bow.[25] Here was a cargo that would realize a high price in Philadelphia and delight the soul of Francis Lewis. John Young, glancing down her manifest, reckoned a fortune from the proceeds of "20 pipes, 20 hogsheads of the finest old Madeira wine; 30 pipes, 10 hogsheads, 20 quarter casks of London market ditto; 70 pipes, 10 hogsheads, 20 quarter casks of New York market ditto; 75 pipes, 100 hogsheads, 100 quarter casks of best cargo ditto. 19 boxes of Poland starch."[26]

While he was nearing Hispaniola, the captain would not sacrifice such a treasure to the Cap François market. Better the risk of the long voyage back to Philadelphia. He removed Gregg and all his hands save two mates and put on board the *Douglass* an ample prize crew. With the prizemaster went a letter to Francis Lewis describing the capture of both the *Tonyn* and the wine brig. They parted company that day, January 16.[27]

Almost a month later on February 13, the *Douglass* sailed up the Delaware to Philadelphia.[28] Lewis hailed her arrival with pleasure and started her through the routine of condemnation and sale with the same rapidity that had marked the conversion of the *Resolution* into Continental dollars. She was libeled against February 24, condemned March 2, and, on March 12 her cargo went under the hammer "near Messrs. Willing and Morris's wharf." The brig was sold at public auction at the London Coffee House that same evening.[29] A worthwhile price was realized for the Madeira, one bidder paying "308 dollars of the New Emission" for one pipe.[30]

With the arrival of the prize in February, the Philadelphia editors had another chance to wax enthusiastic over the accomplishments of John Young. One of them, rushing a hasty paragraph into his paper, reported that "the Saratoga has also taken a schooner from St. Augustine, with lumber, etc. and sent her to Cape Francois."[31] Three days later, he was apologizing to his readers that "In our last we made a mistake respecting the capture of a vessel from St. Augustine by the Saratoga sloop-of-war." His article then continued with a rather complete account of the engagement with the *Tonyn*.[32]

Before many days, the news had reached New York and provoked a ludicrous story in James Rivington's *Royal Gazette*. According to this yarn, the brig from Madeira had arrived off the Delaware capes on December 16, 1780, and had landed one of her owners with a cask of wine for Congress and a suggestion that Captain Gregg would cruise off the coast until he could be captured. "This was afterwards effected by John Young, commander of the Saratoga, privateer," the article explained solemnly, "and thus a fine cargo of Madeira by concerted treachery fell into the rebels possession."[33] The maligned Captain Gregg had friends in New York who made an immediate and indignant call upon the publisher with demands for retraction of the scurrilous charge. Editor Rivington complied with alacrity. On March 10, his *Royal Gazette* addressed "the Public" with the following:

A Paragraph having appeared in the Gazette of the 7th instant, injurious to the character of Captain Archibald Gregg, respecting the capture of the vessel under his command on his passage from Madeira to Charlestown, by the Rebel Ship Saratoga—the Public are requested to suspend their opinion of his conduct until the arrival of the Saratoga and Captain Gregg is released from his confinement on board her, When that Gentleman's loyalty and firm attachment to the British government (well known to many respectable Gentlemen of this city) will convince the Public that the Paragraph alluded to is false and groundless, and only fabricated by some evil-minded person on board the vessel, with a view to claim a part of the cargo for themselves.[34]

That "Rebel Ship Saratoga" and her captain were beginning to annoy the enemy. John Young was very much in the public eye in New York. Tories remembered him from pre-Revolutionary days, and in the past few months he had achieved a reputation. Late in March, the same Rivington's *Royal Gazette* declared triumphantly that "It is reported at Philadelphia, that the Privateer Saratoga, carrying eighteen nine pounders on one deck and commanded by Captain Young, who has been very successful in depredations upon the British commerce, ran into St. Eustatia road after it was in possession of the British squadron, to which it immediately became a prize."[35]

The only truth in the tale was that on February 3, Rodney had taken the Dutch island of St. Eustatius.[36]

In the harbor, His Majesty's ship *Torbay* had seized the *Saratoga*. But it was a seven gun brig bearing that name, loaded with cordage, nails, and provisions and intended for Havana.[37] John Young's *Saratoga* was nowhere near St. Eustatius.

CHAPTER XI

The Last Cruise

FROM the *Saratoga*'s poop at dawn on January 27, John Young spied far ahead through the misty air the twin domes of Morne du Cap, and knew that nestling beneath the encircling mountain was the harbor of his destination, Cap François. Eleven days had elapsed since he had parted from the *Douglass,* and with favorable winds they had skirted the Bahamas, rounded Turk's Island, and now were in waters dominated by the French. Slightly astern, the *Tonyn* sailed in company. Too valuable a vessel to risk to a prize crew without a convoy, she had been under his watchful eye day and night, even though her slower pace had protracted their voyage. Fortunately, during those eleven days no hostile craft had happened upon them.[1] Rodney's men-of-war, which might have barred their progress, were just then refitting far to the southeastward at St. Lucia, after a futile attack upon the French island of St. Vincent.[2]

Passing well to the northward of the clustered isles of the Seven Brothers in the early hours of the morning, the *Saratoga* and *Tonyn* stood in for the cape, took on pilots to negotiate the tricky, narrow channel, and just at noontime dropped anchor in the broad roadstead. Not far away lay the frigate *Confederacy,* and the Philadelphia privateer *Fair American,* Captain Joseph Jakways, a sixteen gun brig.[3] The latter, whose owners had been among those causing the captain so much trouble with the high sheriff of Philadelphia, had arrived five days before after a rapid passage from the Delaware capes.[4]

Whether or not in the days before the Revolution John Young had visited Cap François is not known. He might possibly have been there in the *Tobago* prior to 1768. Certainly, he had never been in the port before as a captain in the Continental navy, and the war years had wrought a great change in and and brought much prosperity to this Paris of the Antilles. In less than a decade it had become the second richest city in all the West Indies, yielding supremacy only to the Spanish port of Havana.[5]

Before he went ashore, Young stood by the rail and appraised the gorgeous scene. Cap François lay spread about him in all its glory, an imposing panorama of splendor. The shore line consisted of a series of quays, all connected by a parklike walk lined with palms, palmettos, and flaming hibiscus. In the background rose the city's solid and substantial edifices of stone interspersed with imposing buildings—great piles of masonry such as the Governor's palace, the massive King's arsenal, the Cathedral, the College of the Jesuits, two cross-tipped convents, and the Theatre Français. Behind all that, to the north, with great flanking arms spreading out east and west, reared the stately green and black heights of Morne du Cap.[6]

But John Young was not there simply to admire the scenery, spectacular as it was. In the early afternoon he was rowed to one of the quays, turned his prize over to the French Admiralty Court for condemnation, paid his respects to the Governor, M. de Belle-combe, and sought out Monsieur Bernard Lavaud, a reputable Cap François merchant who acted as agent for Continental vessels as well as for those on private account. Upon M. Lavaud he would rely to see that his interests in the *Tonyn* were safeguarded.[7]

Back again on the *Saratoga* later in the day, he found a visitor—Captain Seth Harding. The *Confederacy*'s commander told of his own cruise southward, in which one prize had been taken, and related all the gossip of the port—how American merchant captains who were disrespectful to Continental officers had been brought to heel by M. de Bellecombe, and how the Governor now desired to use the American war vessels for convoying purposes. Several days before, the *Confederacy* almost had been sent out to meet and escort in a merchant fleet from Martinique, and now there was brewing a job of giving some American traders a safe offing. Such duty was most acceptable while awaiting cargo.[8]

It seemed, according to Harding, that Carabasse's military stores were not as plentiful as had been sup-posed. Admiral D'Estaing, in 1779, had pre-empted much of the material that had been destined for the Continent.[9] Young made a note to call upon Cara-basse, the Beaumarchais agent, at the earliest oppor-tunity and check Harding's report. The captain quite approved of all the *Confederacy*'s commander had done and no doubt was much interested in the latter's description of a pleasant visit he had made to some of the plantations on the Plaine du Nord. A month or more at the Cap should prove interesting as Harding was most enthusiastic about French hospitality.

Inadvertently, John Young put that hospitality to the acid test the next morning. The day before he had arranged with the Governor for a formal exchange of salutes, and at eight o'clock, he proceeded to carry out his part of the program—twenty-one guns to be fired at minute intervals. The first discharge brought calamity. Unknown to the captain, the gun contained a round shot and a handful of grape. As the detonation echoed back from the mountains, a cloud of dirt leaped high from one of the quays along the shore. Fearful of the consequences but hoping that no one had been injured, Young ordered each gun examined and reloaded. In haste to avoid delay between shots, one of the gun crews sought to reload without springing the weapon. It burst, killing one man and wounding another. In the midst of this mishap, angry port officials boarded the sloop-of-war. A Negro woman had been slain by the cannon ball from the first gun. The captain mollified them and pointed to the destruction wrought on board the *Saratoga*. He promised to call upon the Governor as soon as he could investigate and report the cause of the unfortunate accident. By afternoon he had the story but not the culprits. Some of the prisoners, who had been allowed the freedom of the ship, had found secret opportunity to ram home a 9-pound ball in Number 1 gun. To M. de Bellecombe went Young with the explanation; accompanying him were a number of officers from both the *Saratoga* and *Confederacy*. The matter was settled with no difficulty.[10] The life of one Negro woman was of small moment in Cap François. The days of Toussaint L'Ouverture and Henri Christophe were still years away.

While the record is silent on this point, it is safe to

assume that John Young lost little time in transferring his prisoners into the hands of the French authorities. After that, he called upon Carabasse and received confirmation of the scarcity of military stores. Beaumarchais' agent gave him some details. Not only had D'Estaing's fleet drawn liberally upon the American military supplies in 1779 but the Admiral actually had walked off with "the materials for completely equipping two Frigates of 36 guns."[11] What stores remained would not be in sufficient quantity completely to fill the hold of the *Confederacy*.

Life at Cap François, thereafter, flowed easily—the Theatre Français, dances at the Playhouse, elaborate dinners with cards, a Mustee ball, and other pleasures filled the days. French officers and merchants were indeed hospitable, and the Governor was exceedingly gracious.[12] During this time, the *Tonyn* was condemned, and along with the 9,000 barrels of turpentine in her cargo, she was sold. The proceeds were placed in the hands of M. Lavaud.[13] Meanwhile, the sloop-of-war was docked for graving, and therefore she was not ready to join the *Confederacy* when that vessel left on February 1 to convoy offshore four merchantmen bound for America and then to cruise for several weeks. The frigate *Deane* came into port next day. John Nicholson, whose insubordinate attitude was typical of the three Nicholson brothers, had elected to prolong his cruise from America rather than follow instructions of the Board of Admiralty. Hence, though he had sailed from Baltimore early in November, he had since spent eight profitless weeks scouring West Indian waters for prizes.[14]

When, on February 16, the *Confederacy* sailed

back into the roadstead after a barren two weeks off the coast, the *Saratoga* was ready for sea.[15] By this time, a sizable merchant fleet was assembling and loading at Cap François.[16] M. de Bellecombe estimated there would be eighty or more sail of them ready to depart by mid-March. Approximately half would be destined for America and half for France. Also the Governor was in daily expectation of several French frigates to convoy the contingent bound across the Atlantic.[17] In the interim, he proposed a joint operation for the *Saratoga,* the *Deane,* the *Confederacy,* the privateer *Fair American,* and the French naval brig *Cat.* News had been received of the taking of St. Eustatius by Rodney, which meant the main British fleet still lay in the Leeward Islands. Hence, the Continental vessels might well venture with impunity through the Windward passage and right up to the very shores of the British base at Jamaica.

Of the brief cruise then undertaken, we have but a few fragmentary items of information. They sailed out of Cap François on February 20, and were back in eight days,[18] bringing in with them a rich prize. She was the ship *Diamond,* from St. Kitts to Jamaica. According to one version, she was "a ship of 20 guns" and according to another, "a ship of 32 guns." Both accounts agree that she was ladened deep with some of Rodney's plunder from the former Dutch island. One report goes on to add, that the captors found on board her some two hundred Negro slaves. Confirmation of the *Diamond's* great value can be found in M. Lavaud's account of sales, which showed the Continental share as 265,292.19,11 livres.[19]

By the end of the first week in March, the roadstead of Cap François boasted more than a half hundred sail of merchantmen of all descriptions. Among them were some twenty or more of American register, hailing from New England and North Atlantic ports, and all awaiting a homeward convoy.[20] In the Grand Cafe on one of the quays, where centered the business and shipping interests of the gay city, the merchant skippers gathered daily. The twang of the Yankee mingled with the broader drawl of the Pennsylvanians over many a glass of Maderia or rum. There they drank and yarned—Thorndike, Hobbs, and Green, of Salem; Johnstone and Bickford, of Beverly; Foster and Fling, of Boston; Goodhue, of Newburyport; Babson, of Cape Ann;[21] Smith, Burrows, Pease, and Armitage, of Philadelphia[22]—unsung heroes of the Revolution, who dared the British navy and the horrors of New York prison ships to keep the produce of the West Indies flowing to a beleaguered continent.

M. Carabasse finally had his cargoes ready for the Continental vessels. What remained of the Beaumarchais stores—chiefly clothing for the army—had been divided between the *Confederacy* and the *Deane*. To fill their holds, they took in additional large quantities of sugar, cotton, coffee, and indigo, and M. de Bellecombe placed in the *Deane* some two hundred 13-inch shells for Rochambeau's army. John Young's cargo consisted of sugar, coffee, and rum.[23] All were ready for departure but there was delay. The Governor was still awaiting arrival of his frigates. They came in about March 10, bringing to the rendezvous a dozen ships from Havana.[24] Assembled then in the roadstead and awaiting only a favorable wind were eighty-eight sa of merchantmen—fifty-six destined for France, and thirty-two for America.[25] For convoy there were the French frigates, the Continental ships *Saratoga, Confederacy,* and *Deane,* and the privateer *Fair American.*[26]

John Young, Seth Harding, and John Nicholson paid a formal farewell call upon the Governor before they sailed. He was profusely sorry to bid them good-by and everlastingly grateful for the services they had rendered him. Moreover, he assured them that he was conveying by letter to M. de la Luzerne his very great appreciation, hoping Congress would be informed "that the commanders of the American frigates have, while stationed at the cape, given strong proof of zeal for the common cause," whether in cruising against the enemy or in convoying merchant vessels from Santo Domingo. His missive especially mentioned the captain of the *Saratoga.*[27]

Finally, on March 15, the great fleet stood forth from the harbor of Cap François, and by nightfall the heights of Morne du Cap had sunk beneath the horizon astern. On the port flank of the convoy sailed the *Saratoga.* The course was north by east until they rounded Turk's Island and the Mouchoir Bank and came upon the open sea. By dawn of March 18—the fourth day out—they had reached latitude 22° north, and there the fleet separated. The fifty-six merchant-men bound for France turned their bows eastward, and with their frigate escort were soon hull down in a windy, choppy sea.[28] The vessels intended for the Continent stood due north, herded along by the *Confederacy,* the *Deane,* and the *Fair American,* but *not* by the *Saratoga.*[29]

Sharp eyes in the foretop of the sloop-of-war had

picked up two distant sail to the westward, and John Young had veered from the convoy to investigate. Despite the strong wind and with high seas running, he ordered full canvas clapped on. The *Saratoga's* bow sliced into the waves, which broke across her deck. She heeled to the shocks but raced ahead, gaining upon her quarry, which, it could be plainly seen, was trying to escape, hoping no doubt to gain the safety of some British port in the nearby Bahamas. One officer in the little sloop-of-war marveled at the reckless daring of his captain in flying such a press of sail, yet all of them shared the same venturesome spirit. The excitement of the chase was in the blood of every man on board.[30]

By noon, the merchant fleet had passed from sight to the northeast, and the nearer of the two vessels they were chasing was almost within gunshot. There was slight chance of using 9- or 4-pounders with the sea breaking frequently through the gunports. So the eighteen guns were housed, and would have to stay that way. But John Young saw he had nothing worse than a lightly armed snow-rigged merchant vessel to deal with, so the heavy weather and the housed guns worried him not at all. Within a few more hours, they drew abreast of their first victim and she promptly struck her flag and hauled into the wind. Her name has not been preserved. All we know is that she was a snow bound from South Carolina for London.[31]

Maneuvering nearer and working fast so that he could resume his pursuit of the second quarry, Young launched his longboat over the lee side and sent Midshipman Nathaniel Penfield on board with a prize crew.

"Make sail and follow us," he had told him as the

midshipman slid into the stern sheets of the cockleshell that was to take him across to the prize. "We'll have the other vessel headed before nightfall."

By then it was nearly four o'clock in the afternoon. The weather had been growing steadily worse, yet scarcely had Penfield boarded the captured snow and sent back her crew in the longboat, than the canvas rose again on the *Saratoga*. The midshipman watched the slim sloop-of-war gathering speed and thrilled to the ardor of his captain.

Perhaps in that moment when the swift American vessel lunged again to the chase, John Young may have waved cheerily to his subordinate in the prize. Penfield made no report, however, of any farewell. He turned immediately to obeying the orders given him. Manning the snow hastily, he sent his few hands aloft to bend sail. As they did so, the wind leaped suddenly to almost hurricane velocity. For a moment the prize seemed doomed. She heeled before the mighty blast of wind, then somehow righted herself. Clinging to the yards, the men of the prize worked in frantic haste, reefing in such canvas as had not been torn to shreds. Only when the task was completed and every piece of rigging had been firmly secured was there a moment to see how the chase was progressing.

Nathaniel Penfield peered forward, rubbed his eyes, and stared again, unbelievingly. Far ahead, the quarry was still in flight.

But the *Saratoga* had disappeared.[32]

CHAPTER XII

The Curtain Falls

H ISTORY abounds in coincidences. One such mingled the final days of the northward voyage of the Hispaniola fleet with a major British naval operation. On March 16, off Cape Henry, Admiral Marriott Arbuthnot and Des Touches (the successor to De Ternay, who had died at Newport) fought an inconclusive action, after which the French returned to Rhode Island, and the British retired for repairs to Lynnhaven road within the Virginia capes.[1] Arbuthnot sailed out to sea on April 2, with nine ships of the line and six frigates. Two ships, the *Chatham* and the *Charon,* were detached four days later to scout for the enemy, and three others, the *Pearl,* the *Iris,* and the *Amphitrite,* were ordered south to Cape Fear and Charleston.

Southeast of the Delaware capes, in latitude 38° 30′ north, on April 11, the *Chatham* took a prize, the "Rebel Schooner Amelia, Captain Dickinson," and learned "she was a part of a fleet from St. Domingo bound to Philadelphia under the convoy of the Dean[e] and Confederacy, rebel frigates, and which must be very near us at that period, she having only parted company with them the preceding day."[2] The *Chatham* reported this news a day later, upon rejoining Arbuthnot, and the latter detached the *Roe-*

buck and the *Orpheus* to assist in the search for the "rebels."[3]

Meanwhile, some seven leagues off Charleston on April 13, the *Pearl* and the *Iris* had made out a distant sail, and the latter vessel set off in hot pursuit. After a two-hour chase, she spoke the quarry, which promptly surrendered.[4] The victim was John Young's last prize, the snow from Charleston for London, taken March 18. Nathaniel Penfield and the *Saratoga*'s prize crew were removed, and on April 18 British hands sailed the snow into New York, where the Tory press reported her as "happily re-taken by his Majesty's ships."[5]

During mid-April, the cruising British frigates reaped a rich harvest. Daily between April 12 and 18 one or more of the Cap François fleet fell into the enemy's hands.[6] The climax came on April 19, when the *Roebuck* and the *Orpheus* returned to New York with the *Confederacy*. "The Capture of this ship will be severely felt by the Rebels," a British diarist exulted.[7] Harding had been intercepted off the Virginia capes on April 14 and "prudently" had struck his colors and "submitted without any resistance."[8]

In Philadelphia, the expected Hispaniola fleet was the topic of conversation in early April, but as the month reached the halfway mark with no word, a feeling of alarm arose. Then, on April 17, the vanguard arrived, the ship *Chatham,* Joseph Smith, master. Smith reported the fleet as scattered, and enemy frigates in evidence off the capes.[9] Before another week elapsed matters were brighter, and the *Pennsylvania Packet* on April 24, announced that "Saturday last arrived the Fair American privateer.

Since our last arrived in the Delaware, the St. Domingo and Havannah fleets, consisting of about twenty sail of armed trading vessels, the greatest part of which have entered the harbor."

That same issue listed three letters for John Young lying uncalled for in the Philadelphia postoffice.[10] Later it was learned that the *Deane,* escorting the New England contingent of the fleet, had put safely into Boston on April 16.[11] They heard also of the loss of the *Confederacy.*[12]

But no word came from the *Saratoga.* Joanna Young haunted the wharves, questioned the masters in the Hispaniola fleet, waited and wondered, and then feared. Days became weeks; weeks became months. Nothing was heard. John Young and his gallant crew had vanished from the face of the sea. Francis Lewis resigned in July, and John Brown, the secretary and sole remaining representative of the Board of Admiralty, reviewed certain unfinished naval matters with Congress in August. Among the papers was found the petition to save Young from the clutches of the high sheriff. Across it someone wrote, on August 24, "not to be acted upon." Nothing Congress, nor the Board of Admiralty, nor the high sheriff might ever do could interest John Young again. He was gone forever from the jurisdiction of mundane powers.[13] Brown, however, seems to have clung to some faint hope. In September, when drawing up a list of naval officers, he retained the names of Young and Blaney Allison as in active service. Opposite the captain's name he wrote, "commands the Saratoga"; and opposite Allison's he inscribed, "L^t of the Saratoga now on a Cruize."[14]

Rumors had been current through late spring and summer about the little sloop-of-war. Strangely enough, most of these emanated in New York, where the Tory press continued to grow alarmed whenever they heard the name *Saratoga*. One report, in May, was that she had engaged with and been taken by His Majesty's frigate *Iris* "after a running fight of two hours, in which Captain Young, her commander, was killed." [15] Another, in June, announced she had sailed from Philadelphia "to convoy twelve sail of vessels with flour, &c. to Rhode Island." [16] This, as everybody in Philadelphia knew, was pure poppycock. However, another report arose in August that she had been carried into New York by the *Iris*. [17] Then a Philadelphia newspaper on September 26, reported that "We are assured from good authority, that the ship Saratoga belonging to this state, thought to have been lost at sea, was taken by a British frigate and sent to England. A letter is said to be received from capt. Young dated in St. Thomas." [18]

Of course, the account—like all the others—was spurious; there could be no such letter; but many who had given up all hope were again induced to take heart. Among them were William Livingston, New Jersey's aging Governor, and his two unmarried daughters, the Misses Kitty and Susan. Hard upon the appearance of the article on September 26, the Governor addressed a letter to Benjamin Franklin, American Plenipotentiary in France, asking that a search be instituted in England for his son, Midshipman John Lawrence Livingston, and that every effort be made to secure his exchange. [19]

How anxiety, fear, and hope had animated him and

all his family was described in another letter to Franklin, written by Kitty Livingston on October 19. She hoped the good Doctor would excuse the liberty she was taking in addressing him so soon after her father's letter, but her "great anxiety for a Captive Brother now a Prisoner in some part of England, late a Midshipman on board the Saratoga," encouraged her to add her own appeal.

"It is near a twelve month since my Brother left America," she continued, "& no particulars have reached his family respecting his fate, but the capture of the Ship in which he sailed; for many months we suffered much on his account, those less interested than his relatives, gave up all Idea of ever hearing of the Saratoga—our hope was a remote one, & would admit only of the cruel alternative of capture. . . Any releif that he experiences in consequence of your Excellency's exertions in his favor, will be gratefully acknowledged by his Family & Friends, & particularly so by his affectionate Sister." [20]

As an indication of her complete confidence in the report of the capture of the *Saratoga,* she wrote a letter to her midshipman brother and entrusted it for delivery to Matthew Ridley of Maryland, who was about to depart for France. Ridley then joined in the search for young Livingston but was forced to advise John Jay, husband of the third Livingston sister, that "I can hear nothing of him." [21] Even a sad admission from Mrs. Sarah Jay that the ray of hope that her brother might live "has been greatly obscured by the unsuccessful inquiries of our friends in Europe," [22] would not induce the old Governor to abandon his quest. [23]

Joanna Young, however, accepted the inevitable and had her fears confirmed before the end of that year 1781. Nathaniel Penfield came back from captivity on November 19 and repeated to Mistress Young the tale he told the Agent of Marine in reporting for duty. He had been released upon the surrender of Cornwallis at Yorktown and explained "that he was put on board a Prize taken by the Saratoga . . . and parted with that Ship in a Gale of wind wherein he supposes her to have perished; and the Snow of which he was Prize Master was taken and [he] Carried into York in Virginia which occasioned his being a Captive there."[24] Penfield was granted leave of absence on December 4, and Robert Morris, the Agent of Marine, ordered "his Acco.t of Wages on board the Saratoga to be paid."[25]

Refusing to be beguiled into false hopes by subsequent rumors, Joanna on January 29, 1782, presented her husband's will for probate at the court house in Philadelphia. William Semple and John Pringle, the two who had witnessed Young's signature, went with her to swear to its authenticity.[26] Surviving relatives of a number of other men who had perished in the *Saratoga* also chose the same period to have final testaments probated.[27] Finally, the *Freeman's Journal,* which had been responsible for raising a forlorn hope in the previous September, itself wrote finis to the career of the *Saratoga* on February 13, 1782: "The various reports of the state ship Saratoga having been taken and sent to England, appear to be without foundation—there is all the reason in the world to believe she foundered at sea, as neither the brave man that

commanded her, nor any of his gallant crew have ever
been heard of since she was missing.

> 'She was a fatal and perfidious barque,
> 'Built in the eclipse, and rigg'd with
> curses dark.' " [28]

Two of the officers who had been sent to England
in the *Yarmouth* arrived in Philadelphia before the
end of that month. Joshua Barney, who had escaped
from Mill Prison on May 18, 1781,[29] came overland
from Boston and reported to Robert Morris on February 21.[30] A week later William Brown Faggo put
in his appearance. Faggo had made his escape from
the prison on July 6, 1781, "without Coat or Jacket."[31]
How he got to Philadelphia is not disclosed. He received three months' pay from the Agent of Marine
but was refused prize money by the ex-Continental
Agent. Faggo then reported back to Morris, who "advised him to have recourse to the Law if it were un-
justly withheld but that Congress or myself have
nothing to do in the matter."[32] Faggo departed on
August 27, 1782, for Boston.[33]

The war rolled on to its eventual conclusion. In
March, 1783, when hostilities were at a standstill,
Joanna Young procured a pass through the lines to
New York City.[34] The purpose of her visit is not
clear, but at any rate she was back in Philadelphia by
July 1, when "Joanna Young Widow and relect of
John Young late of Southwark" sold two of the lots
in the Northern Liberties to George Sturmfelts,
grocer.[35] John Paul Jones reappeared then, after a
lapse of more than seven years. He was about to de-

part for France in quest of prize money for the men of the *Bon Homme Richard,* but he took time to solicit Robert Morris in behalf of the widow of his old friend. "Chev^r Paul Jones [called] respecting Prize Money due to Captn John Young," Morris reported, "to which I am a Stranger and referred them to Mr. [John Maxwell] Nesbitt who was agent."[36]

Nesbitt could do nothing about the prizes in Hispaniola, and Joanna Young on March 17, 1784, approached Robert Morris in her own behalf. She asked him for "a Letter for Cape Francois by which to receive Effects of her Husband at that Place." The Agent of Marine explained that the account would have to be adjusted and "then a Letter would be written."[37] It was most disheartening, as Young's estate had been inventoried and appraised by William Semple, and she knew that there was £600 of her husband's money lying in the hands of Bernard Lavaud at Cap François.[38] Four more of the Northern Liberties lots were sold thereafter to John Stroson, a drayman, probably to obtain the wherewithal to live until the money from prizes and back wages could be collected.[39]

Finally, on February 13, 1785, she petitioned Congress for half-pay similar to compensation awarded widows of army officers. She summarized her husband's services to December 15, 1780, "at which time he received Orders to proceed on a Cruise and from which time, neither the Sloop of War the Saratoga nor himself never more was heard of which is now about five Years since." In the belief that "widows of Officers in the Navy are in justice entitled to the same liberality" as army widows, she asked Congress "to

pass a resolve that will entitle her to obtain half pay or
a Sum of Money equivalent thereto both as her ar-
rearage and while she remains Captain Young's widow
or otherwise to relieve her as to your Honour shall
seem just and expedient."[40]

Struggling to hold together the fruits of the Revolution, burdened with debt, and exercising the flimsiest
of national control, Congress resolved on May 16,
1785, "that it is inexpedient to comply with the prayer
of the petitioner."[41] Behind the resolution is a committee report which points out that only the danger of
total dissolution of the army had brought about half-
pay for officers' widows; that some states had submitted to the measure with ill grace; that to extend it
to naval widows might produce bad consequences; and
that, anyhow, the navy man had prize money whereas
the soldier got no booty. In fact, said the committee,
the naval officers "in a less severe service were in a
situation of realizing substantial Riches."[42]

Over the years Governor Livingston had persisted
in his efforts to learn the fate of his son. His habit of
clinging to the slightest straw eventually brought some
scoundrels into the picture, scavengers who sought to
capitalize upon his affliction. One such, Blinkerhorn
by name, claiming to be a seaman just back from captivity in Algiers, approached the Governor late in
1789 with a yarn that could only have been accepted
by an aged man shrewd in most things but gullible in
anything pertaining to the long-lost boy. The *Saratoga,* said Blinkerhorn, had been taken by the Al-
gerians, and Midshipman Livingston for years had
been a captive. The knave claimed to have seen the lad
at work on the fortifications at Algiers and to have

met there two other members of the crew of the sloop-
of-war, Reynolds and Miner.

The old Governor wrote to his son-in-law, John Jay.
Since 1781, Jay had run down every fruitless clue that
William Livingston had supplied. Satisfied that this
newest story was a fabrication throughout, he set to
work nevertheless. An examination of the last muster
roll of the *Saratoga* showed no such names on it as
Reynolds or Miner. Persisting further, Jay located
Nathaniel Penfield, who had been put on board the
snow from Charleston that stormy day in March,
1781. From Penfield he gathered the fate of the little
sloop-of-war, just as the midshipman had related it to
Robert Morris years before—a definite statement that
"The Saratoga is with great probability supposed to
have been lost on the 18th of March, 1781, about four
o'clock in the afternoon of that day." Thus the story
which proved conclusively that John Lawrence Livingston had died with all his shipmates almost nine
years before reached Governor Livingston early in
1790—just a few months, in fact, before he concluded
a long and useful career.[43] John Young's widow died
in June of that same year.[44]

And with them vanished the memory of the exploits
of John Young and his gallant crew in the first
Saratoga.

APPENDIX A

John Young's
Pre-Revolutionary Voyages

THIS list is compiled chiefly from the Custom House records published in the newspapers of New York, Philadelphia, Charleston, and London.

As Mate of the Brig *Tobago*

1768, June 27	Cleared New York for the Grenades
Oct. 17	Entered New York from the Grenades
Dec. 5	Cleared New York for the Grenades
1769, Mar. 6	Entered New York from the Grenades
Apr. 17	Cleared New York for the Grenades
Aug. 3	Entered New York from the Grenades
Oct. 12	Cleared New York for the Grenades
1770, Jan. 15	Entered New York from the Grenades
Apr. 2	Cleared New York for the Grenades
June 21	Entered Philadelphia from the Grenades
Aug. 9	Cleared Philadelphia for the Grenades
Nov. 30	Entered Philadelphia from the Grenades
Dec. 20	Cleared Philadelphia for New York
Dec. 24	Entered New York from Philadelphia
1771, Mar. 4	Cleared New York for the Grenades
June 13	Entered New York from the Grenades
July 11	Cleared New York for the Grenades
Oct. 17	Entered Philadelphia from the Grenades
Nov. 21	Cleared Philadelphia for the Grenades
1772, Mar. 30	Entered New York from the Grenades

As Mate of the Ship *America*

1772, May 11	Cleared New York for Hull, England
Sept. 2	Entered New York from Hull
Oct. 4	Cleared New York for Bristol, England
1773, April 19	Entered New York from Bristol
May 15	Cleared New York for Hull
Sept. 18	Entered New York from Hull

As Master of the Brig *Elizabeth*

1773, Nov. 8	Cleared New York for Charleston
Nov. 15	Entered Charleston from New York
1774, Feb. 4	Cleared Charleston for Gosport, England
Mar. 7	Entered Gosport from Charleston
Mar. 25	Cleared Gosport for Amsterdam
Apr. 20	Entered Amsterdam from Gosport
May 20	Cleared Amsterdam for St. Eustatius
Aug. 29	Entered New York from St. Eustatius
Sept. 12	Cleared New York for Quebec
Dec. 24	Entered New York from Quebec
1775, Jan. 23	Cleared New York for Liverpool, England
May 8	Entered New York from Liverpool
May 29	Cleared New York for London
Sept. 16	Entered New York from London

APPENDIX B

Muster Rolls

THE muster rolls for the *Independence* and *Saratoga* are but partial ones. No complete roster has been found for either vessel.

There is a list in the Historical Section of the Navy Department of the first thirty-one men signed on board the *Independence*. This return has been supplemented by a prize-crew list and an advertisement for deserters, and from several other sources indicated in the narrative.

For the *Saratoga's* muster roll, the principal sources are lists of captured prize crews, taken from the bimonthly returns of several vessels where the prisoners were carried on the rolls at two-thirds rations. Other names have been secured from wills, letters of attorney, and letters or ducements as cited in the text.

Partial Muster Roll of the *Independence*
(July, 1776–June, 1778)

Date of Entry	Men's Names	Quality*	Remarks
1776			
July 23	John Young	Captain	Ordered to Baltimore for court of inquiry, June 18, 1777
Sept. 10	James Robertson	1st Lieut.	On leave, June, 1778
Oct.	James Wilson	2d Lieut.	To sloop *Morris*, Dec. 1776
Sept. 4	William Whitpain	Master	Deserted, May, 1777
Sept. 16	George Brookman	Master's Mate	Discharged, Jan., 1777
. . . . . .	Haley Fletcher	Master's Mate	Deserted, May, 1777
Sept. 26	William Adams	Surgeon	Resigned, Jan. 1777
1777			
Mar. 8	William Russell	Surgeon	On leave, June, 1778
1776			
Sept. 16	Stephen Pater de la Cossade	Midshipman	On leave, June, 1778

*Where "Quality" is left blank, the rating has not been determined.

Date of Entry	Men's Names	Quality*	Remarks
. . . . . .	Andrew Batten	Midshipman	Taken in prize, Sept. 30, 1777
Sept. 28	William Darby	Boatswain	
Sept. 21	William Tucker	Gunner	
Sept. 4	William Hanover	Gunner's Mate	
. . . . . .	Joseph Stout	Carpenter	
Sept. 18	Robert Priest	Carpenter's Mate	
Sept. 5	Stephen Elms	Clerk	Deserted, Jan., 1777
. . . . . .	Peter Deay	Clerk	Deserted, May, 1777
Sept. 18	John Corlett	Cooper	Deserted, May, 1777
Sept. 4	Alexander Riddle	Cook	
Sept. 20	James McCord	Steward	
Sept. 21	Daniel Turner	Able Seaman	
Sept. 21	Ralph Watkins	Able Seaman	
Sept. 24	John Reily	Able Seaman	
Sept. 24	John Colwell	Able Seaman	
Sept. 24	John McKinsy	Able Seaman	
Sept. 24	Charles Moore	Able Seaman	
Sept. 24	James Fisher	Able Seaman	
Sept. 25	Peter Thompson	Able Seaman	
Sept. 25	James Conover	Able Seaman	
. . . . . .	Robert Pritchard	Able Seaman	Deserted, May, 1777
. . . . . .	William McFarland	Able Seaman	Deserted, May, 1777
. . . . . .	Michael Lee	Able Seaman	Deserted, May, 1777
. . . . . .	John Sherwood	Able Seaman	Deserted, May, 1777
. . . . . .	James Elliott(blk)	Able Seaman	Deserted, May, 1777
. . . . . .	John Anderson	Able Seaman	Taken in prize, Sept. 30, 1777
1777			
June 1	Francis Branum	Able Seaman	Taken in prize, Sept. 30, 1777
. . . . . .	William Small	Able Seaman	Taken in prize, Sept. 30, 1777
. . . . . .	John Ogden	Able Seaman	Taken in prize, Sept. 30, 1777
. . . . . .	Patrick Quin	Able Seaman	Taken in prize, Sept. 30, 1777
1776			
Sept. 16	Henry Tucker	Landsman	
Sept. 22	James Black *	Landsman	
Sept. 23	Leonard May	Landsman	
Oct. 1	Edward Crilly	Landsman	
Sept. 16	Nicholas Toub	Boy	
Sept. 23	John Patterson	Boy	

Partial Muster Roll of the *Saratoga*
(February, 1780–March, 1781)

1780			
Feb.	John Young	Captain	Lost in ship, Mar. 18, 1781
July	Joshua Barney	1st Lieut.	Taken in prize, Oct. 11, 1780
July	Blaney Allison	2d Lieut.	Lost in ship, Mar. 18, 1781

Date of Entry	Men's Names	Quality*	Remarks
Nov.	James Pyne	2d Lieut.	Lost in ship, Mar. 18, 1781
July 7	Abraham Van Dyke	Lt. Marines	Resigned, Nov. 1780
Nov.	Hugh Kirkpatrick	Lt. Marines	Lost in ship, Mar. 18, 1781
July	William Brown	Surgeon	Lost in ship, Mar. 18, 1781
July	John Garvin	Master	Taken in prize, Oct. 1780
July	William B. Faggo	Master's Mate	Taken in prize, Oct. 19, 1780
July	John Hackett	Master's Mate	Taken in prize, Oct. 19, 1780
Dec. 6	Joseph Bailey	Master's Mate	Lost in ship, Mar. 18, 1781
July	John L. Livingston	Midshipman	Lost in ship, Mar. 18, 1781
July	Barent Sebring	Midshipman	Lost in ship, Mar. 18, 1781
July	Nathaniel Penfield	Midshipman	Taken in prize, Apr. 1781
July	Samuel Clarkson	Midshipman	Taken in prize, Oct. 19, 1780
July	James McCord	Cooper	Lost in ship, Mar. 18, 1781
July	Prince Gilbert(blk)	Cook	Lost in ship, Mar. 18, 1781
June 5	Charles King	Sergt. Marines	Lost in ship, Mar. 18, 1781
May 1	John Henderson	Clerk	Discharged Aug. 18, 1780
July	James Cunningham	Carpenter's Mate	Taken in prize, Oct. 11, 1781
July	Stephen Thompson	Able Seaman	Lost in ship, Mar. 18, 1781
July	Patrick Green	Able Seaman	Lost in ship, Mar. 18, 1781
July	Thomas Pilkinton	Able Seaman	Lost in ship, Mar. 18, 1781
June 27	Joseph Robinett	Able Seaman	Lost in ship, Mar. 18, 1781
July	William Hamilton		Lost in ship, Mar. 18, 1781
July	Samuel Jones		Lost in ship, Mar. 18, 1781
July	Martin Condern		Lost in ship, Mar. 18, 1781
July	John Jones		Lost in ship, Mar. 18, 1781
July	George Montgomery		Lost in ship, Mar. 18, 1781
July	Anthony Castoff		Deserted, Nov. 25, 1780
July	Richard Mount		Taken in prize, Oct. 11, 1780
July	Anthony Fricker		Taken in prize, Oct. 11, 1780
July	James Stuart		Taken in prize, Oct. 11, 1780
July	George McDonald		Taken in prize, Oct. 11, 1780
July	Arthur Chapman		Taken in prize, Oct. 11, 1780
July	William Fry		Taken in prize, Oct. 11, 1780
July	Joseph Barthlemy		Taken in prize, Oct. 11, 1780
July	William H. Wattles		Taken in prize, Oct. 11, 1780
Nov.	Charles Widdiner		Lost in ship, Mar. 18, 1781
July	John Winsley		Taken in prize, Oct. 19, 1780
July	James Calligan		Taken in prize, Oct. 19, 1780
July	James Gray		Taken in prize, Oct. 19, 1780
July	Samuel Penner		Taken in prize, Oct. 19, 1780
July	William Momon		Taken in prize, Oct. 19, 1780
July	Christopher Cadnan		Taken in prize, Oct. 19, 1780
July	Patrick Phillips		Taken in prize, Oct. 19, 1780
July	James Gibbs		Taken in prize, Oct. 19, 1780
July	Henry Saunders		Taken in prize, Oct. 19, 1780

July	Joseph Craft		Taken in prize, Oct. 19, 1780
July	William Curtis		Taken in prize, Oct. 19, 1780
July	Greenbury Hughes		Taken in prize, Oct. 19, 1780
July	Nimrod Merit		Taken in prize, Oct. 19, 1780
July	John Harper		Taken in prize, Oct. 19, 1780
July	Philip Lotis		Taken in prize, Oct. 19, 1780
July	John McGogin		Taken in prize, Oct. 19, 1780
July	Philip Bradrick		Taken in prize, Oct. 19, 1780
July	Michael Milen		Taken in prize, Oct. 19, 1780
July	Manus Black		Taken in prize, Oct. 19, 1780
July	Joseph Inkley		Taken in prize, Oct. 19, 1780
July	Ebenezer Short		Taken in prize, Oct. 19, 1780
July	Christopher Vandike		Taken in prize, Oct. 19, 1780
July	Moses Newman		Taken in prize, Oct. 19, 1780
July	James Gayton		Taken in prize, Oct. 19, 1780
July	Thomas Hatch		Taken in prize, Oct. 19, 1780
July	Peter Dubois		Taken in prize, Oct. 19, 1780
July	Gabriel Mark		Taken in prize, Oct. 19, 1780
July	Israel Tombs		Taken in prize, Oct. 19, 1780
July	Cornelius Burch		Taken in prize, Oct. 19, 1780
July	Joseph Play		Taken in prize, Oct. 19, 1780
July	John Ross		Taken in prize, Oct. 19, 1780
July	George Robinson		Taken in prize, Oct. 19, 1780
July	James Davison		Taken in prize, Oct. 19, 1780
July	Timothy Collins		Taken in prize, Oct. 19, 1780
July	John Leak		Taken in prize, Oct. 19, 1780
July	Joseph Hill		Taken in prize, Oct. 19, 1780
July	Samuel Bargeman		Taken in prize, Oct. 19, 1780
July	Nicholas Gayton		Taken in prize, Oct. 19, 1780
July	William Bennett		Taken in prize, Oct. 19, 1780
Aug. 15	John Cockshott	Landsman	Lost in ship, Mar. 18, 1781
May 8	James Fricker	Landsman	Discharged, Nov. 5, 1780
May	Jacob Nagle	Landsman	Discharged, Nov. 5, 1780

APPENDIX C

John Young's Prizes

URING his career, Young took nineteen prizes, sixteen while cruising alone and three while in company with other American vessels. Seven of his prizes were retaken, including three most valuable ones. The captures were as follows:

When	Rig	Name	Captain	Cargo	Remarks
			In the *Independence*		
1776					
Oct. 25	Ship	*Sam*	Sam. Richardson	Ivory & Iron	Sent into Phila.
Dec. 15	Brig	*Rebecca*	Hugh Scater		"
1777					
May 11	Schooner	*Mary*	Patrick Bowers	Ballast	Sent into Sinepux- ent
Sept. 7	Brig	*Lovely Peggy*	....		Recaptured
Sept. 14	(vessel's name and rig unknown)		....		Carried into Nantes
			In the *Impertinent*		
1779					
July 16	Sloop of War*	*Harlem*	Josias Rogers	......	Sent into Phila.
Sept.	Ship*	(name unknown)	....	......	Recaptured
			In the *Saratoga*		
1780					
Sept. 12	Snow	*Sarah*	Allen McKinley	Rum	Carried into Phila.
Sept. 25	Sloop	*Elizabeth*	A recapture	Corn & Spars	Sent into Phila.
Oct. 8	Ship	*Charming Molly*	Robert Gill	Rum & Sugar	Recaptured
Oct. 8	Sloop	*Two Brothers*	...... Deane	"	Sent into Phila.

*Taken in company with other American war vessels.

Oct. 10	Ship	*Elizabeth*	David Taylor	Rum & Sugar	Recaptured
Oct. 10	Brig	*Nancy*	Oswald Eve	"	"
Oct. 11	Brig	*Providence*	A recapture	Sugar & Coffee	"
Dec. 21	Ship	*Resolution*	John Laughton	Privateer	Sent into Phila.
1781					
Jan. 9	Ship	*Tonyn*	John Wade	Turpentine & indigo	Carried into Cap François
Jan. 16	Brig	*Douglass*	Archibald Gregg	Maidera wine	Sent into Phila.
Feb. 15	Ship*	*Diamond*	....	Slaves & produce	Carried into Cap François
Mar. 18	Snow	(name unknown)	....	......	Recaptured

Notes

¹ The Board of Admiralty was created by Congress on October 28, 1779. Worthington C. Ford, Gaillard Hunt et al. (eds.), *Journals of the Continental Congress* (Washington, 1909-39), XV, 1216-18.

² The exact date of the keel laying can only be approximated. Earliest mention of the actual building of the new sloop-of-war was on February 22, 1780, when the Board of Admiralty wrote to Charleston, South Carolina, and spoke of "a new ship building here." Marine Committee Letter Book, 263, Library of Congress.

³ The Navy Board of the Middle District was instructed by the Marine Committee on June 18, 1778, to conduct a court of inquiry into the loss of the *Independence*. *Ibid.*, 157. The inquiry was long delayed; probably it was not completed until Young returned from a letter-of-marque cruise in October, 1779. Philadelphia *Pennsylvania Journal and Weekly Advertiser*, October 6, 1779.

⁴ Francis Lewis to President of Congress, December 8, 1779, Papers of the Continental Congress, 78, XIV, 295, Diplomatic and Judicial Records Branch, National Archives, Washington.

⁵ M. V. Brewington, *The Design of Our First Frigates, The American Neptune* (Salem, 1948), 11-25.

⁶ Marine Committee to Navy Board, Eastern Department, August 17, 1779, Marine Committee Letter Book, 228.

⁷ This analysis of the situation of the captains senior to Young is made as of October 2, 1779, the day of the announcement of the appointment of James Nicholson and Thomas Read. By then, of course, John Paul Jones was in command of the *Serapis*, after the *Bon Homme Richard* sank in the famous fight off Flamborough Head, September 23, 1779. Charles Alexander commanded the Pennsylvania brigantine *Active*, and James Josiah, the Pennsylvania ship *Hetty*. Papers of the Continental Congress, 196, I, 100; VII, 69. Isaiah Robinson was in command of the Pennsylvania letter-of-marque ship *General Mercer*. Chatham *New Jersey Journal*, October 19, 1779.

⁸ Board of Admiralty to John Bradford, April 11, 1780, Marine Committee Letter Book, 277.

⁹ Hector McNeill and Thomas Thompson were court-martialed and dismissed from the service in the summer of 1778. *Town's* [Philadelphia] *Pennsylvania Evening Post*, July 14, August 18, 1778. John Burroughs Hopkins and Joseph Olney were suspended by order of the Marine Committee, May 20, 1779. Marine Committee Letter Book, 215. Dudley Saltonstall was awaiting court-martial in Boston. *Ibid.*, 249. John Manley

had been captured in the privateer *Jason* on September 30, 1779. Boston *Gazette,* November 29, 1779.

[10] Marine Committee to Navy Board Eastern Department, October 6, 1779, Marine Committee Letter Book, 241.

[11] Boston *Gazette,* September 27, 1779. A little later, Hacker waived his rank and joined the Continental frigates assigned to Charleston, South Carolina, as a lieutenant. Marine Committee Letter Book, 297.

[12] The last reference to Thomas Grennell's active service lists him as commanding the frigate *Congress,* in the Hudson River in the fall of 1777. *Ibid.,* 97. In a naval list for September, 1781, he is recorded as "unemployed-Connecticut." Papers of the Continental Congress, 37, 473.

[13] Ford *et al.* (eds.), *Journals of Congress,* November 20, 1776, VI, 970.

[14] Navy Board of the Middle District to Wharton & Humphreys, July 1, 1779, in Joshua Humphreys Papers, Correspondence, 1775-1831, Historical Society of Pennsylvania.

[15] Report, Board of Treasury, December 13, 1779, Papers of the Continental Congress, 136, III, 896. Dimensions of the *Saratoga* are in the Humphrey Papers in the private collection of M. V. Brewington, Cambridge, Maryland. The "Spirketing" referred to by Humphreys is the inside planking between the water-ways and the ports of a vessel.

[16] The Congressional members were William Ellery of Rhode Island, and James Forbes of Maryland. The secretary was John Brown, who had been secretary of the Marine Committee for the entire period of its existence. Ford *et al.* (eds.), *Journals of Congress,* December 3, 8, 1779, XV, 1344, 1366.

[17] Board of Admiralty to President of Congress, January 3, 1780, Papers of the Continental Congress, 37, 169.

[18] Marine Committee to Seth Harding, September 17, 1779, Marine Committee Letter Book, 235; William Carmichael to President of Congress, October 25, 1779, in Francis Wharton (ed.), *Revolutionary Diplomatic Correspondence of the United States* (Washington, 1889), III, 393.

[19] Eugene Parker Chase (trans.), *Our Revolutionary Forefathers, The Letters of François, Marquis de Barbé Marbois,* 1779-85 (New York, 1929), 128.

[20] M. de la Luzerne to President of Congress, November 17, 1779, m Wharton (ed.), *Revolutionary Diplomatic Correspondence,* III, 408-410.

[21] Chase (trans.), *Letters of Marbois,* 128.

[22] Company receipts, July 17, 1776, in Papers of John Cadwalader, I, 35, Historical Society of Pennsylvania.

[23] Both Young and Semple signed a petition for appointment of William Brown as auctioneer, December 1, 1779, in Simon Gratz Autograph Collection, Convention, I, 14, Historical Society of Pennsylvania.

[24] Deed Book D, 2-490, 10-186, 11-147, 22-74, Recorder of Deeds, Philadelphia.

[25] Northern Liberties State Tax, 1781, in William Henry Egle (comp.), *Pennsylvania Archives,* (3d ser., Harrisburg, 1896, 1897), XVI, 74.

[26] Marine Committee to Navy Board, Eastern Department, November 10, 1779, Marine Committee Letter Book, 245.

[27] Board of Admiralty to Jonathan Trumbull, December 18, 1779, *ibid.,* 252.

[28] *Id.* to Samuel Nicholson, January 31, 1780, *ibid.,* 259.

29 Elbridge Gerry to James Warren, January 7, 1780, in Worthington Chauncey Ford (ed.), *The Warren-Adams Letters* (vols. 72 and 73 of Massachusetts Historical Society *Collections*, Boston, 1917, 1925), II, 123.

30 Board of Admiralty to Congress, January 7, 1780, Marine Committee Letter Book, 256.

31 Report, Board of Admiralty, January 24, 1780, Papers of the Continental Congress, 37, 175.

32 Board of Admiralty to John Langdon, February 15, 1780, Marine Committee Letter Book, 262.

33 John Jay to President of Congress, December 24, 1779, in Wharton (ed.), *Revolutionary Diplomatic Correspondence*, III, 436-45.

34 Board of Admiralty to Navy Board, Eastern Department, February 22, 1780, Marine Committee Letter Book, 265.

35 *Id.* to *id.*, April 18, 1780, *ibid.*, 280.

Chapter II

1 *Appleton's Cyclopaedia of American Biography* (New York, 1918), 504, 505.

2 Evidence that Young sailed in the *Tobago* in the summer of 1768 is provided by a listing of letters which remained uncalled for in the New York post office, July 5, 1768, a week after that brig had cleared for one of her numerous voyages to the Grenades. The list included three letters for him. New York *Gazette and the Weekly Mercury*, July 25, 1768.

3 *Names of Persons for whom Marriage Licenses were issued by the Secretary of the Province of New York, Previous to 1784. Edited by Order of Gideon Tucker, Secretary of State* (Albany, 1860), 476; Samuel S. Purple (ed.), *Records of the Reformed Dutch Church in New Amsterdam and New York, Marriages from 11 December, 1639, to 26 August, 1801* (New York, 1890), I, 235.

4 Petition of Joanna Young, February 23, 1785, Papers of the Continental Congress, 42, VIII, 467.

5 John Young's will, August 8, 1780, Will Book S, 63, 61, Register of Wills, Philadelphia.

6 This appraisal of John Young's education is based upon the few letters written by him which have survived. The best of these is one written in 1777 to the American Commissioners in France in Benjamin Franklin Papers, VII, 149, American Philosophical Society, Philadelphia. He did misspell certain words with uniform consistency, and occasionally ventured a disconcerting vowel where none might be expected, but his handwriting was legible. His way of stating matters succinctly left nothing to conjecture.

7 John Jay to William Livingston, January 25, 1790, in Henry Johnston (ed.), *The Correspondence and Public Papers of John Jay* (New York, 1890-92), III, 383, 384; Inventory of the Estate of John Young Esquire Late Commander of the *Saratoga* Ship of War, March 1782, Will Book S, 63, 61, Register of Wills, Philadelphia.

8 See Appendix A for voyages in the *Tobago*, the *America*, and the *Elizabeth* prior to the Revolution.

9 "List of Letters remaining in the General Postoffice, New York, July 6, 1772," includes one for "John Young of the Ship America," in New York *Gazette and the Weekly Mercury*, July 13, 1772.

10 Admiralty Secretary, Miscellanea, Ships' Passes, Class 7, 98, 2305, Public Records Office. An advertisement in the Charleston *South Carolina Gazette*, December 6, 1773, referred to the *Elizabeth* as "a fine, stout, new vessel."

11 *Marine Society of the City of New York Membership List* (New York, 1913), 97. Young joined the Society, October 18, 1773, one week after the quarterly meeting which was held on the evening of October 11. New York *Gazette and the Weekly Mercury*, October 4, 1773.

12 London *Chronicle*, from January 8 to January 11, 1774; New York *Gazette and the Weekly Mercury*, November 15, 1773.

13 Philadelphia *Pennsylvania Gazette*, December 22, 1773.

14 News of the Boston Tea Party was contained in a dispatch dated December 20, 1773 and printed in the January 21 section of the London *Chronicle*, a tri-weekly newspaper, January 20-22, 1774.

15 New York *Gazette and the Weekly Mercury*, September 7, 1774.

16 London *Chronicle*, June 27-29; June 29-July 1; and July 11-13, 1775.

17 "Extract of a Letter from Philadelphia, May 5, 1776," Boston *Gazette*, May 20, 1776.

18 Ford *et al.* (eds.), *Journals of Congress*, May 6, 13, 22, 1776, IV, 328, 251, 279.

19 Return List, Sloop *Independence*, July 23-October 1, 1776, in Revolutionary Naval Papers, Bureau of Rolls and Records, Navy Department, Washington (hereinafter referred to as Return List, *Independence*). It has been claimed for John Paul Jones that on August 8, 1776, he received the first naval commission as captain after the adoption of the Declaration of Independence. It may be noted, however, that John Young's commission was dated July 23, 1776.

20 Ford *et al.* (eds.), *Journals of Congress*, October 10, 1776, VI, 861.

21 Willing, Morris & Co. to William Bingham, September 27, 1776, in Robert Morris Papers, Accession 1805, Library of Congress.

22 Secret Committee to William Bingham, September 24, 30, 1776, in Simon Gratz Autograph Collection, Uncatalogued, and Case 1, Box 19, Historical Society of Pennsylvania.

23 "Extract of a Letter from Barbadoes, November 20, 1776," in London *Public Advertiser*, January 28, 1777; Philadelphia news dispatch and libel against ship *Sam* in *Pennsylvania Gazette*, November 27, 1776.

24 Robert Morris to George Washington, December 21, 1776; *id.* to John Hancock, December 21, 1776; receipt of Hugh Peden, December 21, 1776; George Washington to Robert Morris, December 25, 1776, all in Peter Force (comp.), *American Archives* (5th ser., Washington, 1853), III, 1330, 1331, 1419, 1420.

25 Robert Morris to William Bingham, February 12, 1777, in Ferdinand Dreer Autograph Collection, Historical Society of Pennsylvania.

26 *Town's Pennsylvania Evening Post*, May 15, 1777.

27 Libel against schooner *Mary*, June 23, 1777, Admiralty Court, Baltimore, Box 1, Folder 14, Hall of Records, Annapolis.

28 "Extract of a Letter from Sinepuxent, August 8, 1777," in *Pennsylvania Journal and Weekly Advertiser*, August 13, 1777; Paul Wentworth's

Port News, about October 17, 1777, in B. F. Stevens (comp.), *Facsimiles of Manuscripts in European Archives Relating to America* (London, 1889-95), No. 274; George Washington to Israel Putnam, August 11, 1777, in George Washington Papers, Library of Congress.

29 List of American Prisoners confined in Forton Prison, December 29, 1777, in Franklin Papers, II, 29, Historical Society of Pennsylvania; George Lupton (Vanzandt) to William Eden, October 15, 1777, in Stevens (comp.), *Facsimiles*, No. 204.

30 George Cartling (Paul Wentworth) to Lord Suffolk, October 6, 1777, *ibid.*, 270.

31 Journal of Arthur Lee, September 29, 1777, in Richard Henry Lee, *Life of Arthur Lee* (Boston, 1829), I, 335; Silas Deane to John Young, November 8, 1777, in Charles Isham (ed.), *The Deane Papers*, II, *Collections* of the New York Historical Society (1887-91), 212, 213.

32 The last reference to the *Independence* as a sloop is in the Journal of Arthur Lee, September 29, 1777, in Lee, *Life of Arthur Lee*. The next reference to her rating as "the Brigtn Independence" is in the log of the *Ranger* for December 16, 1777. Bureau of Rolls and Records, Navy Department, Washington, (hereinafter cited as *Ranger's* Log).

33 Narrative of Jonathan Austin, in Edward Everett Hale and E. E. Hale, Jr., *Franklin in France* (Boston, 1887), I, 157-59; John Paul Jones to American Commissioners, December 4, 1777, in Franklin Papers, VII, 129, American Philosophical Society.

34 John Paul Jones to John Young, November 18, 1778, in John Paul Jones MSS., Library of Congress.

35 John Young to the American Commissioners, December 16, 1777, in Franklin Papers, American Philosophical Society; Benjamin Franklin and Silas Deane to John Young, December 2, 1777, in Isham (ed.), *Deane Papers*, II, 261, 262.

36 Journal of Arthur Lee, December 29, 1777, January 8, 1778, in Lee, *Life of Arthur Lee*, I, 371, 372, 375-78.

37 John Paul Jones to Silas Deane, February 26, 1778, in Franklin Papers, XLVIII, 139, American Philosophical Society; *id.* to Jonathan Williams, Jr., February 15, 1778, Papers of the Continental Congress, 168, I, 31.

38 *Ranger's* Log, February 25, 1778.

39 John Paul Jones to John Young, November 18, 1778, in John Paul Jones MSS.

40 Memorial of Thomas Bell, May 20, 1783, Papers of the Continental Congress, 137, II, 627.

41 John Bondfield to American Commissioners, July 4, 1778, in Franklin Papers, X, 91, American Philosophical Society.

42 Marine Committee to Hewes, Smith and Allen, February 20, 1779, Marine Committee Letter Book, 198.

43 Thomas Bell to John Paul Jones, November 3, 1778, in John Paul Jones MSS.

44 James Nicholson to the Marine Committee, April 2, 1778, in *Town's Pennsylvania Evening Post*, May 28, 1778.

45 William Bell Clark, *Captain Dauntless, The Story of Nicholas Biddle of the Continental Navy* (Baton Rouge, 1949), 235-42.

46 *Town's Pennsylvania Evening Post*, May 1, 1778.

[47] Boston *Independent Chronicle*, April 16, 1778.

[48] William Ellery to William Whipple, May 31, 1778, in Peter Force Transcripts, Library of Congress.

[49] Marine Committee to John Young, June 18, 1778, Marine Committee Letter Book, 158.

[50] Thomas Bell to John Paul Jones, November 3, 1778, in John Paul Jones MSS.

[51] Supply and State Tax Returns, 1779, in Egle (comp.), Pennsylvania Archives (3d ser.) XV, 140; *MacPherson's Directory for the City and Suburbs of Philadelphia* (Philadelphia, 1785).

[52] Supply and State Tax Returns, 1779, in Egle (comp.), Pennsylvania Archives (3d ser.) XV, 140.

[53] Silas Deane to President of Congress, July 10, 1778, in Wharton (ed.), *Revolutionary Diplomatic Correspondence*, II, 640-42; Marine Committee to Navy Board, Eastern Department, July 11, 24, 29, 1778, and to Comte d'Estaing, July 12, 17, August 12, Marine Committee Letter Book, 162-65, 167, 171. For a clear exposition of D'Estaing's frustrated maneuvers on the Atlantic coast in 1778, see A. T. Mahan, *The Influence of Sea-Power upon History, 1660-1783* (Boston, 1894), 359-65.

[54] Papers of the Continental Congress, 196, II, 61.

[55] Joanna Young's will, Will Book U, 40, 48, Register of Wills, Philadelphia.

[56] Inventory of the Estate of John Young Esquire.

[57] Papers of the Continental Congress, 196, VIII, 33; *Pennsylvania Gazette*, October 6, 1779.

[58] John Barry to Matthew Irwin, July 16, 1778, in Charles Roberts Autograph Collection, Haverford College Library.

[59] *Dunlap's* [Philadelphia] *Pennsylvania Packet, or the General Advertiser*, July 22, 1779; *Pennsylvania Gazette*, July 23, 1779.

[60] Joseph Dashiell to Maryland Delegates in Congress, July 28, 1779, Papers of the Continental Congress, 78, VII, 271.

[61] *Pennsylvania Gazette*, October 6, 1779; Board of Admiralty to James Nicholson, April 17, 1780, Marine Committee Letter Book, 280.

CHAPTER III

[1] Board of Admiralty to Hewes, Smith and Allen, April 7, 1780, Marine Committee Letter Book, 275.

[2] The earliest record of the name *Saratoga* is in the list of vessels of the Continental navy attached to a letter from the Board of Admiralty to Benjamin Franklin, March 28, 1780. A copy of this letter, without attachment, is in Marine Committee Letter Book, 272, and another copy is in Papers of the Continental Congress, 193, 828, also without attachment. The list, however, was copied by William Temple Franklin into the American Legation Letter Book, 1780, in Benjamin Franklin Papers, Library of Congress.

[3] Board of Admiralty to Navy Board, Eastern Department, April 7, 1780, Marine Committee Letter Book, 274.

⁴ Francis Lewis to President of Congress, March 21, 1780, Papers of the Continental Congress, 78, XIV, 309.

⁵ Report, Board of Admiralty, April 11, 1780, *ibid.*, 37, 223.

⁶ Ford *et al.* (eds.), *Journals of Congress*, April 12, 1780, XVI, 353.

⁷ Mary Barney in *Biographical Memoir of the Late Commodore Joshua Barney* (Boston, 1832), 89, listed "16 nine pounders." A British captain reported "20 Guns, nine & sixes" (Public Records Office, Rodney Papers, Bundle 14). A New York newspaper mentioned "eighteen nine pounders on one deck" (*Rivington's* [New York] *Royal Gazette*, March 31, 1781). However, the log of H.M.S. *Swift* for October 19, 1780, in recording the capture of one of the *Saratoga's* prizes, gave the armament which was most likely correct, since it came from the lips of the *Saratoga's* prizemaster. The log read, "sixteen Nine and two four pounders" (Admiralty, Captains' Logs, Class 51, Public Records Office).

⁸ Board of Admiralty to Navy Board, Eastern Department, April 18, 1780, Marine Committee Letter Book, 280.

⁹ Francis Lewis to Benjamin Franklin, March 28, 1780, *ibid.*, 270.

¹⁰ Board of Admiralty to Navy Board, Eastern Department, April 7, 1780, *ibid.*, 274.

¹¹ "Extract of a letter from a gentleman at Charlestown, January 29 [1780]," in Boston *Independent Chronicle*, April 6, 1780.

¹² Board of Admiralty to James Nicholson, April 17, 1780, Marine Committee Letter Book, 280.

¹³ Private Journal of Captain Joseph Hardy, in James L. Howard, *Seth Harding, Mariner* (New Haven, 1930), 223, 230, 250, 255-56.

¹⁴ Board of Admiralty to Navy Board, Eastern Department, May 12, 1780, Marine Committee Letter Book, 285.

¹⁵ *Id.* to Samuel Nicholson, May 12, 1780, *ibid.*, 285.

¹⁶ *Id.* to James Nicholson, May 22, 1780, *ibid.*, 288.

¹⁷ New York *Gazette and the Weekly Mercury*, May 22, 1780.

¹⁸ M. de la Luzerne to President of Congress, May 16, 1780, in Wharton (ed.), *Revolutionary Diplomatic Correspondence*, III, 683-85.

¹⁹ Report, Committee on Conference with the French Minister, May 24, 1780, *ibid.*, III, 699-701.

²⁰ Ford *et al.* (eds.), *Jounals of Congress*, May 27, 1780, XVII, 469.

²¹ Board of Admiralty to Jonathan Trumbull, and *id.* to President of New Hampshire and Governor of Massachusetts, May 30, 1780, Marine Committee Letter Book, 289-91.

²² *Id.* to Nathaniel Shaw, Jr., May 22, 1780, *ibid.*, 287.

²³ *Id.* to Navy Board, Eastern Department, June 16, 1780, *ibid.*, 294.

²⁴ Navy Board, Middle District to Board of Admiralty, June 5, 1780, Papers of the Continental Congress, 78, XIV, 337.

²⁵ Board of Admiralty to Navy Board, Eastern Department, June 16, 1780, Marine Committee Letter Book, 294.

²⁶ Navy Board, Eastern Department, to Board of Admiralty, June 14, 1780, in Letter Book, Navy Board, Eastern Department, 120, Library of Congress.

²⁷ "Extract of a letter from a person lately from New York, dated August 10 [1780]," Boston *Independent Chronicle*, September 7, 1780.

²⁸ Board of Admiralty to James Nicholson, June 30, 1780, Marine Committee Letter Book, 298.

29 Ford *et al.* (eds.), *Journals of Congress,* June 24, 1780, XVII, 556.
30 Board of Admiralty to M. Carabasse, June 1, 1780, Marine Committee Letter Book, 293.
31 *Id.* to Navy Board, Eastern Department, May 30, 1780, *ibid.,* 291.

CHAPTER IV

1 Theodore Sedgwick, Jr., *A Memoir of the Life of William Livingston* (New York, 1835), 345.
2 Barney's biographers include Ralph D. Paine, *Joshua Barney, a Forgotten Hero of Blue Water* (New York, 1924), and Hulbert Footner, *Sailor of Fortune, The Life and Adventures of Commodore Barney, U.S.N.* (New York, 1940).
3 William Frederick Adams (comp.), *A Few Facts in Connection with the "Life of Commodore Joshua Barney"* (Springfield, Mass., 1912).
4 Memorial of Joshua Barney, July 26, 1780, Papers of the Continental Congress, 41, I, 301.
5 Barney, *Biographical Memoir,* 1-83.
6 Memorial of Joshua Barney, July 26, 1780, Papers of the Continental Congress, 41, I, 301.
7 Barney, *Biographical Memoir,* 82, 83.
8 Memorial of Joshua Barney, July 26, 1780, Papers of the Continental Congress, 41, I, 301.
9 Ford *et al.* (eds.), *Journals of Congress,* July 27, 1780, XVII, 675.
10 *Ibid.,* August 7, 1780, p. 702.
11 Francis Allison to Robert Allison, August 20, 1776, "Notes and Queries," in *Pennsylvania Magazine of History and Biography,* XXVIII (1904), 379.
12 Muster roll, Ship *Montgomery,* 1776, 1777, in John Blair Linn (comp.), *Pennsylvania Archives* (2d ser., Harrisburg, 1879), I, 339.
13 List of Officers in the Navy of the United States, September, 1781, Papers of the Continental Congress, 37, 433.
14 Danske Dandridge, *American Prisoners of the Revolution* (Charlottesville, Va., 1911), 450; court-martial proceedings, November 25, 1777, Papers of the Continental Congress, 78, II, 307-11.
15 List of Officers in the Navy of the United States, September, 1781, Papers of the Continental Congress, 37, 433.
16 George Washington to Board of Admiralty, May 29, 1780, *ibid.,* 37, 423.
17 Captain's commission for Abraham Van Dyke, July 8, 1780, *ibid.,* 37, 426; Ford *et al.* (eds.), *Journals of Congress,* July 14, 1780, XVII, 612.
18 Report, Board of Admiralty, July 15, 1780, Papers of the Continental Congress, 37, 415.
19 Ford *et al.* (eds.), *Journals of Congress,* July 21, 24, 1780, XVII, 650, 651, 661.
20 W. B. Aiken, *Beekman and Van Dyke Genealogies* (New York, 1912), 200-26; John C. Van Dyke, *The Raritan, Notes on a River and a Family* (New Brunswick, 1915).

21 George Washington to Board of Admiralty, May 29, 1780, Papers of the Continental Congress, 37, 423.

22 Force (comp.), *American Archives*, I, 918; II, 522.

23 [Elias Boudinot], *Journal, or Historical Recollections of American Events During the Revolutionary War* (Philadelphia, 1894), 15, 16.

24 George Washington to Board of Admiralty, May 29, 1780, Papers of the Continental Congress, 37, 423.

25 *Pennsylvania Magazine of History and Biography*, XV (1891-92), 242.

26 William Brown's will, July 28, 1780, Will Book S, 74, 71, Register of Wills, Philadelphia.

27 Letter of attorney, William Brown, July 28, 1780, in "Notes and Queries," *Pennsylvania Magazine of History and Biography*, XXVII (1903), 115.

28 "Extract of a letter, dated Mill Prison (Plymouth), February 24, 1781," in *Dunlap's Pennsylvania Packet or the General Advertiser*, June 23, 1781.

29 Ezra Stearns, *Genealogical and Family History of New Hampshire* (New York, 1908), III, 1073, 1074.

30 "The Diary of Master Joseph Tate," in *New England Historical and Genealogical Register*, LXXIII (1919), 305.

31 "People's Certificates that were on board the Drake May [16] 1778," in Franklin Papers, LXI, 99, American Philosophical Society.

32 *Ranger*'s Log, March 23, 1780; Roll of the Officers and Men belonging to the Continental Ship of War *Ranger*, 1780, Misc. Collections, Box 15A, Historical Society of Pennsylvania.

33 *Pennsylvania Gazette*, June 28, 1780.

34 Mary Faggo to Thomas Bradford, November 15, December 28, 1780, in Thomas Bradford Papers, Correspondence, III, 135, 151, Historical Society of Pennsylvania.

35 *Boston Births from 1700 to 1800*, City Document No. 43 (Boston, 1849), 296.

36 "Extract of a letter dated Mill Prison (Plymouth), February 24, 1781," in *Dunlap's Pennsylvania Packet or the General Advertiser*, June 23, 1781.

37 John Hackett to Thomas Jones, February 23, 1781, Papers of the Continental Congress, 78, XIII, 233-37.

38 Thomas Jones to John Sullivan, June 30, 1781, *ibid.*, 232.

39 Linn (comp.), *Pennsylvania Archives* (2d ser.), I, 298.

40 *Ibid.*, 355.

41 Court martial, John Hackett, January 13, 1777, in Ferdinand Dreer Autograph Collection, Historical Society of Pennsylvania.

42 Sedgwick, *Livingston*, 345.

43 Edwin Brockholst Livingston, *The Livingstons of Livingston Manor* (New York, 1910), 536.

44 Kitty Livingston to Mrs. John Jay, July 10, 1780, in Johnston (ed.), *Jay Papers*, I, 375-77.

45 William Livingston to John Lawrence Livingston, April 19, 1780, in Sedgwick, *Livingston*, 345-47.

46 Peter Roome Warner (comp.), *Descendants of Peter Willemse Roome* (New York, 1883), 160.

⁴⁷ The genealogical table of the Penfield family was furnished by the late Louis C. Penfield of Evanston, Illinois.

⁴⁸ Deposition, Captain Walter Young, H.M.S. *Alcide*, October 16, 1780, New York Prize Papers, High Court of Admiralty, Public Records Office, London.

⁴⁹ John Hall and Samuel Clarkson, *Memoirs of Matthew Clarkson of Philadelphia, 1735-1800, and of His Brother Gerardus Clarkson, 1737-1790* (Philadelphia, 1890).

⁵⁰ Marine Commitee to Seth Harding, September 17, 1779, Marine Committee Letter Book, 235.

⁵¹ Kitty Livingston to Mrs. John Jay, July 10, 1780, in Johnston (ed.), *Jay Papers*, I, 375-77.

⁵² Samuel Clarkson's claim for pay, No. 2647, General Accounting Office, Washington.

⁵³ Board of Admiralty to Navy Board, Eastern Department, June 16, 1780, Marine Committee Letter Book, 294.

⁵⁴ *Id.* to President of Congress, June 7, 1780, Papers of the Continental Congress, 37, 251; Ford *et al.* (eds.), *Journals of Congress*, June 7, 1780, XVII, 492.

⁵⁵ Petition of Philip Lyons, November 20, 1780, Papers of the Continental Congress, 37, 537.

⁵⁶ Petition of Seth Harding and John Young to Board of Admiralty, quoted in Howard, *Seth Harding*, 128, 129.

⁵⁷ Report, Board of Admiralty, July 10, 1780, Papers of the Continental Congress, 37, 261; Ford *et al.* (eds.), *Journals of Congress*, July 11, 1780, XVII, 603.

⁵⁸ Will of Stephen Thompson, July 19, 1780, Will Book U, 30, 80, Register of Wills, Philadelphia; Advertisement for a deserter in *Pennsylvania Gazette*, December 13, 1780.

⁵⁹ Minutes, Supreme Executive Council of Pennsylvania, July 19, 1780, in Samuel Hazard (ed.), *Pennsylvania Colonial Records* (Harrisburg, 1851-53), XII, 427.

⁶⁰ For partial roll of the *Saratoga*, see Appendix B.

⁶¹ *Rivington's* [New York] *Royal Gazette*, September, 23, 1780.

⁶² Ford *et al.* (eds.), *Journals of Congress*, July 25, 1780, XVII, 666.

Chapter V

¹ M. de la Luzerne to President of Congress, July 22, 1780, in Wharton (ed.), *Revolutionary Diplomatic Correspondence*, III, 875.

² *Id.* to *id.*, July 25, 1780, *ibid.*, 881, 882.

³ Ford *et al.* (eds.) *Journals of Congress*, July 25, 1780, XVII, 663.

⁴ Report, Board of Admiralty, undated, Papers of the Continental Congress, 37, 503.

⁵ William Ellery to President of Congress, June 26, 1780, *ibid.*, 78, VIII, 342.

⁶ Board of Admiralty to Navy Board, Eastern Department, August 4, 1780, Marine Committee Letter Book, 310.

[7] Ford *et al.* (eds.), *Journals of Congress*, July 26, 1780, XVII, 669.

[8] Report, Board of Admiralty, July 21, 1780, Papers of the Continental Congress, 37, 273.

[9] Board of Admiralty to President of Congress, August 14, 1780, Marine Committee Letter Book, 316.

[10] *Pennsylvania Gazette*, August 9, 1780; Diary of George Nelson of Philadelphia, August 8, 1780, in Historical Society of Pennsylvania.

[11] John Young's will.

[12] Ford *et al.* (eds.), *Journals of Congress*, July 19, 1780, XVII, 645.

[13] *Ibid.*, November 1, 1779, XV, 1232.

[14] Henry Laurens to Committee of Foreign Affairs, February 14, 24, 1780, in Wharton (ed.), *Revolutionary Diplomatic Correspondence*, III, 494, 516, 517.

[15] Ford *et al.* (eds.), *Journals of Congress*, July 7, 1780, XVII, 594.

[16] *Ibid.*, July 19, 1780, XVII, 645.

[17] Board of Admiralty to John Young, August 11, 1780, Marine Committee Letter Book, 313.

[18] *Id.* to James Nicholson, August 11, 1780, *ibid.*, 312.

[19] *Id.* to John Young, August 11, 1780, *ibid.*, 313.

[20] *Id.* to George Washington, August 14, 1780, *ibid.*, 315.

[21] George Washington to Board of Admiralty, August 6, 1780, Papers of the Continental Congress, 37, 311.

[22] Board of Admiralty to George Washington, August 14, 1780, Marine Committee Letter Book, 315.

[23] *Id.* to President of Congress, August 14, 1780, *ibid.*, 316.

[24] "Narrative of Henry Laurens," in *Collections* of the South Carolina Historical Society, I (1857), 18, 19.

[25] Board of Admiralty to Henry Fisher, August 19, 1780, Marine Committee Letter Book, 318.

[26] Chevalier de Ternay to George Washington, August 10, 1780, in Washington Papers; Minutes, French Legation, August 22, 1780, in William S. Mason Collection, Yale University Library.

[27] Ford *et al.* (eds.), *Journals of Congress*, August 19, 1780, XVII, 748.

[28] Board of Admiralty to M. Carabasse, August 19, 1780, Marine Committee Letter Book, 318.

[29] *Id.* to John Young, August 19, 1780, *ibid.*, 317.

[30] Report, Board of Admiralty, August 19, 1780, Papers of the Continental Congress, 37, 295.

[31] *Pennsylvania Journal and Weekly Advertiser*, July 12, 19, 26, August 2, 16, 30, 1780.

[32] Report, Board of Admiralty, August 24, 1780, with endorsements, Papers of the Continental Congress, 37, 299.

[33] Report, Board of Admiralty, August 19, 1780, *ibid.*, 37, 295.

[34] Upon the report of August 24, the Secretary of Congress noted, "Left to the discretion of the Admiralty."

[35] Board of Admiralty to George Washington, August 31, 1780, Marine Committee Letter Book, 322.

[36] *Id.* to James Nicholson, September 2, 1780, *ibid.*, 323.

[37] De B. Randolph Keim, *Rochambeau: A Commemoration by the Congress of the United States of America of the Services of the French Auxiliary Forces in the War of Independence* (Washington, 1907), 342.

Chapter VI

[1] Navy Board, Middle District, to Pennsylvania Supreme Executive Council, September 14, 1780, in Samuel Hazard (comp.), *Pennsylvania Archives* (1st ser., Harrisburg, 1852-56), VIII, 553.

[2] "Narrative of Henry Laurens," *loc. cit.*

[3] Henry Laurens to President of Congress, September 14, 1780, in Wharton (ed.), *Revolutionary Diplomatic Correspondence*, IV, 56.

[4] Deposition, George Keppel, October 6, 1780, in Stevens (comp.), *Facsimiles*, No. 923. This is one of the rare instances where a document identifies the American flag with thirteen stars.

[5] List of prizes taken on the Newfoundland station, May 5-September 10, 1780, London *Courant*, October 4, 1780.

[6] "Supernumeries carried for rations," Muster roll, H.M.S. *Vestal*, September 3, 1780, Admiralty, Class 36, 9529, Public Records Office.

[7] Captain's log, H.M.S. *Vestal*, September 3, 1780, *ibid.*, Class 51, 1034.

[8] Henry Laurens to President of Congress, September 14, 1780, in Wharton (ed.), *Revolutionary Diplomatic Correspondence*, IV, 56.

[9] Deposition, George Keppel, October 6, 1780, in Stevens (comp.), *Facsimiles*, No. 923.

[10] John Adams to President of Congress, December 28, 1780, in Wharton (ed.), *Revolutionary Diplomatic Correspondence*, IV, 213.

[11] Captain's log, H.M.S. *Vestal*, September 9, 1780, Admiralty, Class 51, 4231, Public Records Office.

[12] John Steel to Commanding Officer at New York, September 22, 1780, Rodney Papers, Bundle 14, Public Records Office.

[13] Captain's log, H.M.S. *Keppel*, September 9, 1780, Admiralty, Class 51, 4231, Public Records Office.

[14] *Rivington's* [New York] *Royal Gazette*, September 23, 1780.

[15] John Steel to Commanding Officer at New York, September 22, 1780, Rodney Papers, Bundle 14.

[16] Navy Board, Middle District, to Pennsylvania Supreme Executive Council, September 14, 1780, in Hazard (comp.), *Pennsylvania Archives* (1st ser.), VIII, 553.

[17] Captain's log, H.M.S. *Keppel*, September 9, 1780, Admiralty, Class 51, 4231, Public Records Office.

[18] John Steel to Commanding Officer at New York, September 22, 1780, Rodney Papers, Bundle 14, Public Records Office.

[19] George Brydges Rodney to Marriott Arbuthnot, October 8, 1780, Admiralty, Rodney Papers XX, 9, 7, Public Records Office.

[20] Board of Admiralty to Navy Board, Eastern Department, September 19, 1780, Marine Committee Letter Book, 332.

[21] *Pennsylvania Journal and Weekly Advertiser*, September 20, 1780.

[22] Board of Admiralty to Navy Board, Eastern Department, September 12, 1780, Marine Committee Letter Book.

[23] *Id.* to Joseph Reed, September 13, 1780, *ibid.*, 330.

[24] Minutes, Pennsylvania Supreme Executive Council, September 14, 1780, in Hazard (ed.), *Pennsylvania Colonial Records*, XII, 482.

[25] Libel against Snow *Sarah*, in *Dunlap's Pennsylvania Packet, or the General Advertiser*, September 19, 1780.

²⁶ Advertisement of sale of Snow *Sarah* and cargo, *ibid.*, September 23, 1780.

²⁷ *Rivington's* [New York] *Royal Gazette*, September 13, 1780.

²⁸ Francis Vinton Greene, *The Revolutionary War* (New York, 1911), 217-19.

CHAPTER VII

¹ Board of Admiralty to Navy Board, Eastern Department, September 5, 1780, Marine Committee Letter Book, 324.

² *Id.* to John Barry, September 5, 1780, *ibid.*, 328.

³ *Id.* to Navy Board, Eastern Department, September 12, 1780, *ibid.*, 329.

⁴ Chevalier de Ternay to George Washington, August 10, 1780, in Washington Papers.

⁵ Navy Board, Middle District, to Pennsylvania Supreme Executive Council, September 14, 1780, in Hazard (comp.), *Pennsylvania Archives* (1st ser.), VIII, 553.

⁶ Board of Admiralty to John Young, September 14, 1780, Marine Committee Letter Book, 331.

⁷ *Id.* to James Nicholson, September 14, 1780, *ibid.*, 331.

⁸ Minutes, Pennsylvania Supreme Executive Council, September 14, 1780, in Hazard (ed.), *Pennsylvania Colonial Records*, XII, 482.

⁹ John Young to Navy Board, Middle District, September 16, 1780, in Bradford Papers, British Naval Prisoners, Correspondence, II.

¹⁰ George Brydges Rodney to Philip Stephens, September 15, 1780, in Dorothy C. Barck (ed.), *Letter Books and Order Book of Admiral Lord Rodney* I, *Collections* of the New York Historical Society (1932), 9-11.

¹¹ *Id.* to Marriott Arbuthnot, October 19, 1780, *ibid.*, 43-46.

¹² Captains' logs, H.M.S. *Triton* and H.M.S. *Guadaloupe*, Admiralty Class 51, 1013, part v; 422, part viii, Public Records Office.

¹³ George Brydges Rodney to Marriott Arbuthnot, September 21, 1780, in Barck (ed.), *Rodney Letter Books*, I, 15; *id.* to Philip Affleck, October 2, 1780, *ibid.*, I, 21.

¹⁴ *Pennsylvania Gazette*, September 27, 1780; Richard Langdon to Samuel Langdon, October 5, 1780, printed in the December 4 section of the London *Chronicle*, December 2-5, 1780.

¹⁵ Libel against Sloop *Elizabeth*, in *Dunlap's Pennsylvania Packet, or the General Advertiser*, September 30, 1780.

¹⁶ New York *Gazette and the Weekly Mercury*, October 2, 1780.

¹⁷ Libel against Sloop *Elizabeth*, in *Dunlap's Pennsylvania Packet, or the General Advertiser*, September 30, 1780.

¹⁸ Charleston news dispatch, October 12, 1780, *Pennsylvania Journal and Weekly Advertiser*, November 29, 1780.

¹⁹ George Brydges Rodney to Philip Stephens, October 28, 1780, in Barck (ed.), *Rodney Letter Books*, I, 55-58.

²⁰ George Montagu to George Brydges Rodney, October 15, 1780, *ibid.*, 36, 37.

²¹ George Brydges Rodney to Philip Stephens, October 28, 1780, *ibid.*, 55-58.

[22] *Id.* to Marriott Arbuthnot, October 19, 1780, *ibid.*, 15.

[23] *Id.* to Philip Stephens, October 13, 1780, *ibid.*, 35.

[24] Account of repairs to *Saratoga*, November 1, 1780, in Joshua Humphreys Papers, Day Book, 1773-1781, Historical Society of Pennsylvania.

[25] Captain's log, H.M.S. *Iris*, Admiralty, Class 51, 4224, Public Records Office.

[26] Barney, *Biographical Memoir*, 84-86.

[27] Captain's log, H.M.S. *Intrepid*, Admiralty, Class 51, 475, Public Records Office.

[28] Barney, *Biographical Memoir*, 84-86.

[29] *Pennsylvania Journal and Weekly Advertiser*, October 18, 1780.

[30] *Pennsylvania Gazette*, October 25, 1780.

[31] Muster Table, H.M.S. *Intrepid*, October 1-November 30, 1780, Admiralty, Class 36, 8504, Public Records Office.

[32] Libel against Sloop *Two Brothers*, October 20, 1780, *Dunlap's Pennsylvania Packet, or the General Advertiser*, October 21, 1780.

[33] Barney, *Biographical Memoir*, 84-86.

[34] John Hackett to Thomas Jones, February 14, 1781, Papers of the Continental Congress, 78, XIII, 233-37.

[35] New York *Gazette and the Weekly Mercury*, October 23, 1780.

[36] *Dunlap's Pennsylvania Packet, or the General Advertiser*, October 24, 1780.

[37] New York *Gazette and the Weekly Mercury*, October 23, 1780.

[38] John Hackett to Thomas Jones, February 14, 1781, Papers of the Continental Congress, 78, XIII, 233-37.

[39] Parole of David Taylor, October 14, 1780; of James Savage and Henry Jackson, October 21, 28, 1780, in Bradford Papers, British Naval Prisoners, Paroles, 119, 120, 127.

[40] Exchange list, British naval prisoners, September 3-November 25, 1780, *ibid.*, British Naval Prisoners, Correspondence, I, 70; paroles of Thomas Lyons and Thomas Hadley, October 22, 1780, *ibid.*, Paroles, 121.

[41] John Hackett to Thomas Jones, February 14, 1781, Papers of the Continental Congress, 78, XIII, 233-37.

[42] Muster roll, H.M.S. *Swift*, October, 1780, Admiralty, Class 36, 9963, Public Records Office.

[43] John Hackett to Thomas Jones, February 14, 1780, Papers of the Continental Congress, 78, XIII, 233-37.

[44] Deposition, William Grindley, undated, Prize Papers, New York, High Court of Admiralty, Class 32, 428, Public Records Office.

[45] Deposition, Joseph Bennet, undated, *ibid.*

[46] Deposition, Walter Young, October 16, 1780, *ibid.*

[47] Master's log, H.M.S. *Alcide*, Admiralty, Class 52, 1557, Public Records Office.

[48] Paroles of William Thackstone and William Grindley, October 28, 1780, in Bradford Papers, British Naval Prisoners, Paroles, 125, 217.

[49] Captains' logs, H.M.S. *Triton* and H.M.S. *Guadaloupe*, Public Records Office.

[50] Deposition, William Grindley, undated, Public Records Office.

[51] Board of Admiralty to Thomas Bradford, October 14, 1780, in British Naval Prisoners, Correspondence, II.

C H A P T E R   V I I I

¹ Robert Morris' Diary in the Office of Finance, June 11, 1782, Library of Congress (hereafter cited as Morris' Diary); Barney, *Biographical Memoir*, 84-86; Board of Admiralty to Thomas Bradford, October 14, 1780, Bradford Papers.

² *Pennsylvania Gazette*, September 27, 1780; New York *Gazette and the Weekly Mercury*, October 2, 1780; Richard Langdon to Nathaniel Thwing, October 5, 1780, printed in the December 4 section, London *Chronicle*, December 2-5, 1780.

³ Susan Livingston to Mrs. John Jay, October 21, 1780, in Johnston (ed.), *Jay Papers*, I, 376.

⁴ Exchange list, British naval prisoners, September 3-November 25, 1780, in Bradford Papers, British Naval Prisoners, Correspondence I, 70.

⁵ Board of Admiralty to Thomas Bradford, October 14, 1780, *ibid.*, Correspondence, II.

⁶ *Ibid.*, Paroles, 119-31.

⁷ Account of repairs to *Saratoga*, November 1, 1780, in Humphreys Papers, Pennsylvania Historical Society.

⁸ *Dunlap's Pennsylvania Packet, or the General Advertiser*, October 24, 1780.

⁹ *Pennsylvania Gazette*, October 25, 1780.

¹⁰ *Town's Pennsylvania Evening Post*, May 15, 1777.

¹¹ John Jay to William Livingston, January 25, 1790, in Johnston (ed.), *Jay Papers*, III, 383, 384.

¹² New York news dispatch, October 13, 1780, *Dunlap's Pennsylvania Packet, or the General Advertiser*, October 21, 1780; libel against Sloop *Two Brothers, ibid.*

¹³ New York news dispatch, October 30, 1780, *Pennsylvania Journal and Weekly Advertiser*, November 8, 1780.

¹⁴ Master's log H.M.S. *Alcide*, October 11, 1780, High Court of Admiralty, Assignment Books, 1777-1783, XLIX, 92; VI, 356-59, Public Records Office; "The Adv. Gen¹. ex rel of Walter Young Esq vs Brig° Providence and Cargo, October 16-November 8, 1780," High Court of Admiralty, Prize Papers, New York, Class 32, 428, *ibid.*

¹⁵ Captain's log H.M.S. *Raleigh*, October 11, 1780, Admiralty, Class 51, 762, Public Records Office; Captain's log, H.M.S. *Intrepid*, October 11, 1780, *ibid.*, 475.

¹⁶ Muster roll, H.M.S. *Intrepid*, October, 1780, *ibid.*, Class 36, 8504, *ibid.*

¹⁷ Barney, *Biographical Memoir*, 85.

¹⁸ New York *Gazette and the Weekly Mercury*, October 23, 1780.

¹⁹ John Hackett to Thomas Jones, February 14, 1781, Papers of the Continental Congress. The British frigate first noted by Hackett was probably the *Alcide*. His letter called it the *Alfred*, but that vessel was not then on the American station.

²⁰ Captain's log H.M.S. *Swift*, October 19, 1780, Admiralty, Class 51, 964, Public Records Office.

²¹ Muster roll, H.M.S. *Swift*, October, 1780, *ibid.*, Class 36, 9963, *Ibid.*

[22] George Brydges Rodney to Philip Stephens, October 28, 1780, in Barck (ed.), *Rodney Letter Books,* I, 54-58.

[23] *Id.* to Commissioners for Sick and Hurt Seamen, October 12, 28, 1780, *ibid.,* I, 33, 34, 63, 64.

[24] *Id.* to Philip Stephens, October 28, 1780, *ibid.,* I, 54-58.

[25] Muster Roll, H.M.S. *Royal Oak,* November-December, 1780, Admiralty, Class 36, 9522, Public Records Office.

[26] George Brydges Rodney to Philip Stephens, October 28, 1780, Barck (ed.), *Rodney Letter Books,* I, 54-58.

[27] "Extract of a letter from a Captain of a vessel belonging to this city [Philadelphia] dated Mill-Prison, in England, Feb. 23, 1781," *Pennsylvania Gazette,* July 11, 1781.

[28] George Brydges Rodney to Philip Stephens, December 10, 1780, in Barck (ed.), *Rodney Letter Books,* I, 90-94.

[29] *Id.* to Skeffingham Lutwidge, November 14, 1780, Admiralty I, Captains' Letters, 3056, Sec. 2, No. 8, Public Records Office.

[30] Skeffingham Lutwidge to Philip Stephens, December 26, 1780, *ibid.,* No. 6.

[31] Barney, *Biographical Memoir,* 86, 87.

[32] "Extract of a letter dated Mill Prison (Plymouth), February 24, 1781," *Dunlap's Pennsylvania Packet, or the General Advertiser,* June 23, 1781.

[33] Barney, *Biographical Memoir,* 87, 88.

[34] "Mill Prison Diary of William Widger of Marblehead," June 9, 16, 1781, in *Historical Collections* of the Essex Institute, LXIII (1932), 313, 314.

Chapter IX

[1] Report, Board of Admiralty, November [?], 1780, Papers of the Continental Congress, 37, 503.

[2] *Ibid.,* November 4, 1780, *ibid.,* 37, 513; Ford *et al.* (eds.), *Journals of Congress,* November 7, 1780, XVIII, 1027.

[3] Report, Board of Admiralty, November 6, 1780, Papers of the Continental Congress, 37, 517.

[4] Account of repairs to the *Saratoga,* November 1, 1780, Humphreys Papers, Historical Society of Pennsylvania.

[5] *Dunlap's Pennsylvania Packet, or the General Advertiser,* September 23, 1780.

[6] Libel against Sloop *Two Brothers,* and advertisement of sale of Sloop *Elizabeth* and cargo, *ibid.,* October 21, November 4, 1780.

[7] Report, Board of Admiralty, November 24, 1780, Papers of the Continental Congress, 37, 529.

[8] Report, Congressional Committee, November 25, 1780, *ibid.,* 28, 125.

[9] *Dunlap's Pennsylvania Packet, or the General Advertiser,* October 24, 1780.

[10] William Vernon to William Ellery, November 10, 1780, in "Papers of William Vernon and the Navy Board," Rhode Island Historical Society *Collections,* VIII (1901), 268.

[11] Report, Board of Admiralty, November 6, 1780, Papers of the Continental Congress, 37, 517.

[12] Memorial of James Nicholson, October 21, 1780, *ibid.*, 37, 525.

[13] Report, Board of Admiralty, November 13, 1780, *ibid.*, 37, 521.

[14] *Pennsylvania Journal and Weekly Advertiser*, November 22, 1780.

[15] Ford *et al.* (eds.), *Journals of Congress*, November 27, 1780, XVIII, 1097.

[16] *Ibid.*, October 25, 1780, XVIII, 978.

[17] William Vernon to William Ellery, November 10, 1780, in "Papers of William Vernon," *loc. cit.*

[18] Navy Board, Eastern Department, to John Barry, November 10, 1780, Papers of the Continental Congress, 193, 599.

[19] Inventory of the Estate of John Young Esquire.

[20] Exchange list of British Prisoners, September 3–November 25, 1780, Bradford Papers.

[21] List of Officers of the United States Navy, September, 1781, Papers of the Continental Congress, 37, 433.

[22] "A list of the Commissioned Officers who served in the Navy of the United States in the late War, March 18, 1794," Navy Miscellany, Library of Congress.

[23] A. S. Salley (ed.), *Journal of the Commissioners of the Navy of South Carolina, October 9, 1776–March 1, 1779; July 22, 1779–March 23, 1780* (Columbia, 1912, 1913), I, 42, 100, 105.

[24] London *Public Advertiser*, April 29, 1778.

[25] Salley (ed.), *Journal of Commissioners*, I, 171.

[26] *Ibid.*, 209.

[27] *Rivington's* [New York] *Royal Gazette*, May 1, 1779.

[28] Salley (ed.), *Journal of Commissioners*, II, 45.

[29] *Ibid.*, 59.

[30] "A List of the Rebel Ships of War taken or destroyed in the Harbour of Charles Town [May 14, 1780]," London *Courant*, June 16, 1780.

[31] Memorial of James Pyne and Charles McCarthy, July 18, 1780, Papers of the Continental Congress, 41, VIII, 132.

[32] Ford *et al.* (eds.), *Journals of Congress*, July 19, 1780, XVII, 643.

[33] Report, Board of Admiralty, October 25, 1780, endorsed upon memorial of James Pyne and Charles McCarthy, Papers of the Continental Congress, 41, VIII, 132.

[34] Claim No. 2298, General Accounting Office, Washington.

[35] Exchange list of British prisoners, September 3–November 17, 1780, Bradford Papers.

[36] "Notes and Queries," in *Pennsylvania Magazine of History and Biography*, XXVII (1903), 115.

[37] *Pennsylvania Gazette*, December 13, 1780.

[38] Advertisement of sale of Sloop *Elizabeth*, in *Dunlap's Pennsylvania Packet, or the General Advertiser*, November 4, 1780.

[39] Hardy Journal, in Howard, *Seth Harding*, 256.

[40] Hazard (ed.), *Pennsylvania Colonial Records*, XII, 535, 537.

[41] Joseph Reed to Pennsylvania Delegates in Congress, November 30, 1780, in Hazard (comp.), *Pennsylvania Archives* (1st ser.), VIII, 643.

[42] Ford *et al.* (eds.), *Journals of Congress*, December 1, 1780, XVIII, 1113.

⁴³ *Ibid.*, December 12, 1780, XVIII, 1143, 1149.

⁴⁴ Hardy Journal, in Howard, *Seth Harding*, 258.

⁴⁵ *Ibid.*, 257.

⁴⁶ Report, Board of Admiralty, December 9, 1780, Papers of the Continental Congress, 37, 543.

⁴⁷ Board of Admiralty to Thomas Bradford, December 4, 1780, in Bradford Papers, British Naval Prisoners, Correspondence, II.

⁴⁸ Report, Board of Admiralty, December 9, 1780, Papers of the Continental Congress, 37, 543.

⁴⁹ Privateer bonds, *ibid.*, 196, II, 110; III, 18; IV, 108; X, 195.

⁵⁰ Report, Board of Admiralty, December 9, 1780, *ibid.*, 37, 543.

⁵¹ John Almon (ed.), *The Remembrancer* (London, 1780), XI, 160.

⁵² Report, Board of Admiralty, December 9, 1780, Papers of the Continental Congress, 37, 543.

⁵³ *Rivington's* [New York] *Royal Gazette*, January 3, 1781.

⁵⁴ Navy Board, Eastern Department, to Board of Admiralty, April 18, 1781, Letter Book, Navy Board, Eastern Department.

⁵⁵ M. de la Luzerne to President of Congress, May 25, 1781, in Wharton (ed.), *Revolutionary Diplomatic Correspondence*, IV, 434, 435.

⁵⁶ Petition of Joanna Young, February 23, 1785, Papers of the Continental Congress, 42, VIII, 467.

Chapter X

¹ Hardy Journal, in Howard, *Seth Harding*, 260.

² Seth Harding was commissioned, September 25, 1778, Ford *et al.* (eds.), *Journals of Congress*, September 25, 1778, XII, 951.

³ Hardy Journal, in Howard, *Seth Harding*, 260.

⁴ *Ibid.*, 258-59.

⁵ *Ibid.*, 260.

⁶ *Rivington's* [New York] *Royal Gazette*, January 3, 1781.

⁷ Hardy Journal, in Howard, *Seth Harding*, 260.

⁸ Bradford Papers, Lists of Prisoners, British Army and Navy, 70.

⁹ *Pennsylvania Gazette*, January 10, 1781.

¹⁰ Libel against Ship *Resolution*, in *Dunlap's Pennsylvania Packet, or the General Advertiser*, January 6, 1781.

¹¹ Parole of John Mullet, November 27, 1780, in Bradford Papers, American Naval Prisoners, Paroles, 23.

¹² *Rivington's* [New York] *Royal Gazette*, January 6, 1781; Charleston *South Carolina Royal Gazette*, January 11, 1781.

¹³ Henry Fisher to Caesar Rodney, January 1, 1781, in Bradford Papers, British Naval Prisoners, Correspondence, II.

¹⁴ Paroles of Richard Pender, James Laughton, Josiah Childs, February, 1781, *ibid.*, British Naval Paroles, 136, 137.

¹⁵ Johnston (ed.), *Jay Papers*, III, 383, 384.

¹⁶ Libel against Ship *Resolution*, in *Dunlap's Pennsylvania Packet, or the General Advertiser*, January 6, 1781; advertisements of sale and of completion of sale of Ship *Resolution*, in *Pennsylvania Journal and Weekly Advertiser*, January 13, 31, 1781.

¹⁷ Hardy Journal, in Howard, *Seth Harding*, 260.

[18] "Extract of a letter from St. Augustine, dated April 2 [1781]," *Dunlap's Pennsylvania Packet, or the General Advertiser,* May 1, 1781.

[19] *Ibid.,* February 27, 1781.

[20] *Pennsylvania Gazette,* February 28, 1781.

[21] *Pennsylvania Journal and Weekly Advertiser,* February 28, 1781.

[22] "Extract of a letter from St. Augustine," *Dunlap's Pennsylvania Packet, or the General Advertiser,* May 1, 1780.

[23] *Ibid.,* February 27, 1781.

[24] *Pennsylvania Journal and Weekly Advertiser,* February 28, 1781.

[25] *Dunlap's Pennsylvania Packet, or the General Advertiser,* February 14, 1781.

[26] Advertisement of sale of Brig *Douglass* and cargo, *ibid.,* March 6, 1781.

[27] Bradford Papers, Lists of Prisoners, British Army and Navy, 70.

[28] *Dunlap's Pennsylvania Packet, or the General Advertiser,* February 14, 1780.

[29] Libel against Brig *Douglass, ibid.,* February 27, 1781.

[30] John Gibson to President of Congress, April 27, 1781, Papers of the Continental Congress, 78, X, 319.

[31] *Dunlap's Pennsylvania Packet, or the General Advertiser,* February 14, 1781.

[32] *Ibid.,* February 27, 1781.

[33] *Rivington's* [New York] *Royal Gazette,* March 7, 1781.

[34] *Ibid.,* March 10, 1781.

[35] *Ibid.,* March 31, 1781.

[36] W. M. James, *The British Navy in Adversity* . . . (London, 1926), 255, 256.

[37] Rodney Papers, 20, 15, Public Records Office.

Chapter XI

[1] Hardy Journal, in Howard, *Seth Harding,* 272.

[2] James, *The British Navy in Adversity,* 253, 254.

[3] Bond of privateer *Fair American,* December 9, 1780, Papers of the Continental Congress, 196, IV, 108.

[4] Hardy Journal in Howard, *Seth Harding,* 271-72.

[5] James Breck Perkins, *France in the American Revolution* (Boston, 1911), 357, 358.

[6] Charles Mackenzie, *Notes on Haiti* (London, 1830), 152-54.

[7] Inventory of the Estate of John Young Esquire.

[8] Hardy Journal, in Howard, *Seth Harding,* 270.

[9] *Ibid.,* 143, 144.

[10] *Ibid.,* 273.

[11] Ford *et al.* (eds.), *Journals of Congress,* June 24, 1780, XVII, 555, 556.

[12] Hardy Journal in Howard, *Seth Harding,* 272-73.

[13] "General Account of Prizes, 1781," in Robert Morris, *A Statement of the Accounts of the United States of America during the Administration of the Superintendent of Finance* (Philadelphia, 1785).

[14] Hardy Journal, in Howard, *Seth Harding,* 274.

[15] *Ibid.,* 159.

16 William Affleck's intelligence, March 24, 1781, enclosed in Joshua Rowley to Philip Stephens, undated, Admiralty, Secretary in Letters, 242, 204, Public Records Office.

17 Salem news dispatch, March 20, 1781, *Dunlap's Pennsylvania Packet, or the General Advertiser*, April 14, 1781.

18 Salem news dispatch, March 20, 1781, *New York Gazette and the Weekly Mercury*, April 2, 1781.

19 *Pennsylvania Gazette*, March 28, 1781; *Pennsylvania Journal and Weekly Advertiser*, March 28, 1781; "General Account of Prizes, 1781," *loc. cit.*

20 New York *Gazette and the Weekly Mercury*, April 16, 1781.

21 Salem news dispatch, April 7, 1781, *Pennsylvania Journal and Weekly Advertiser*, May 2, 1781.

22 "Port Arrivals," *The Freeman's* [Philadelphia] *Journal or North American Intelligencer*, April 25, May 2, 1781.

23 New York *Gazette and the Weekly Mercury*, April 23, 1781.

24 *Dunlap's Pennsylvania Packet, or the General Advertiser*, April 24, 1781.

25 Salem news dispatch, April 17, 1781, Hartford *Connecticut Courant*, April 24, 1781.

26 *Rivington's* [New York] *Royal Gazette*, April 18, 1781.

27 M. de la Luzerne to President of Congress, May 9, 1781, Papers of the Continental Congress, 37, 463; Minutes, French Legation, May, 1781, William S. Mason Collection.

28 Salem news dispatch, April 7, 1781, *Pennsylvania Journal and Weekly Advertiser*, May 2, 1781.

29 New York *Gazette and the Weekly Mercury*, April 16, 1781.

30 Johnston (ed.), *Jay Papers*, III, 383, 384.

31 New York news dispatch, April 19, 1781, *Pennsylvania Gazette*, May 2, 1781.

32 Morris' Diary, November 19, 1781.

C H A P T E R   XII

1 James, *The British Navy in Adversity*, 270-74.

2 New York *Gazette and the Weekly Mercury*, April 16, 1781; *Diary of Frederick Mackenzie* (Cambridge, 1929, 1930), II, 506.

3 *Journal of Lieutenant, later Rear Admiral Bartholomew James, R.N.* (London, 1896), 108, 109.

4 Captain's log, H.M.S. *Pearl*, April 13, 1781, Admiralty, Class 51, 675, Public Records Office.

5 New York news dispatch, April 19, 1781, *Pennsylvania Gazette*, May 2, 1781.

6 New York *Gazette and the Weekly Mercury*, April 16, 23, 1781; *Rivington's* [New York] *Royal Gazette*, April 18, 1781.

7 *Diary of Frederick Mackenzie*, April 19, 1781, II, 508, 509.

8 New York *Gazette and the Weekly Mercury*, April 23, 30, 1781.

9 *Pennsylvania Journal and Weekly Advertiser*, April 18, 1781.

10 *Dunlap's Pennsylvania Packet, or the General Advertiser*, April 24, 1781.

[11] New Haven *Journal,* May 2, 1781.

[12] *Dunlap's Pennsylvania Packet, or the General Advertiser,* May 2, 1781.

[13] Francis Lewis to President of Congress, July 12, 1781, Papers of the Continental Congress, 78, XIV, 445; Report, Board of Admiralty with endorsement, August 24, 1781, "not to be acted upon," *ibid.,* 37, 543.

[14] "List of Officers of the United States Navy, September, 1781."

[15] New York *Gazette and the Weekly Mercury,* May 5, 1781.

[16] *Rivington's* [New York] *Royal Gazette,* June 9, 1781.

[17] Anonymous to David Forman, August 13, 1781, Washington Papers.

[18] *The Freeman's* [Philadelphia] *Journal, or North American Intelligencer,* September 26, 1781.

[19] Sedgwick, *Livingston,* 348.

[20] Catherine W. Livingston to Benjamin Franklin, October 19, 1781, in Franklin Papers, No. 32, Acquisition 1946, Historical Society of Pennsylvania.

[21] Matthew Ridley to John Jay, December 10, 1781, in Johnston (ed.), *Jay Papers,* II, 162.

[22] Sarah Jay to William Livingston, January 31, 1782, *ibid.,* 170, 171.

[23] Sedgwick, *Livingston,* 348.

[24] Morris' Diary, November 19, 1781.

[25] *Ibid.,* December 4, 1781.

[26] John Young's will, proved, January 29, 1782.

[27] See Will Book S, 59, 58; 74, 71; 81, 79, and 83, 82, Register of Wills, Philadelphia.

[28] *The Freeman's* [Philadelphia] *Journal, or North American Intelligencer,* February 13, 1782. The editor quoted John Milton's *Lycidas,* line 100.

[29] "Mill Prison Diary of William Widger of Marblehead," May 18, 1781, *loc. cit.,* 311.

[30] Morris' Diary, February 21, 1782.

[31] *Ibid.,* February 27, 1782.

[32] *Ibid.,* June 17, 1782.

[33] Minutes, Pennsylvania Supreme Executive Council, August 27, 1782, in Hazard (ed.), *Pennsylvania Colonial Records,* XIII, 356.

[34] *Ibid.,* March 6, 1783, 524.

[35] Deed Book D-10, Recorder of Deeds, Philadelphia.

[36] Morris' Diary, October 14, 1783.

[37] *Ibid.,* March 17, 1784.

[38] Inventory of Estate of John Young Esquire.

[39] Deed Book D-11, 147, Recorder of Deeds, Philadelphia.

[40] Petition of Joanna Young, February 23, 1785, Papers of the Continental Congress, 42, VIII, 467.

[41] Ford *et al.* (eds.), *Journals of Congress,* May 16, 1785, XXVIII, 362.

[42] Committee report on petition of Joanna Young, March 22, 1785, Papers of the Continental Congress, 19, VI, 603.

[43] Johnston (ed.), *Jay Papers,* III, 383, 384.

[44] Joanna Young's will, proved June 26, 1790.

Bibliography

WHILE all the authorities consulted are listed here, the principal source material has been found in manuscript form and in collections of printed letters.

Printed Documents and Document Collections

- *Boston Births from 1700 to 1800, City Document No. 43* (Boston, 1849).

Clark, Walter (comp.). *State Records of North Carolina,* 30 vols. (Winston, 1890-1915).

- *Delaware Archives,* 4 vols. (Wilmington, 1911-16).

Egle, William Henry (comp.). *Pennsylvania Archives,* Third Series, 30 vols. (Harrisburg, 1896, 1897).

Force, Peter (comp.). *American Archives,* Fifth Series, 3 vols. (Washington, 1856-63).

Ford, Worthington Chauncey, Gaillard Hunt *et al.* (eds.). *Journals of the Continental Congress, 1774-1789,* 34 vols. (Washington 1904-37).

- Hazard, Samuel (ed.). *Pennsylvania Colonial Records,* 16 vols. (Harrisburg, 1851-53).

—————— (comp.). *Pennsylvania Archives,* First Series, 12 vols. (Harrisburg, 1852-56).

Jenckes, Joseph (comp.). *Civil and Military Lists of Rhode Island* (Providence, 1901).

Lincoln, Charles Henry (comp.). *A Calendar of John Paul Jones Manuscripts in the Library of Congress* (Washington, 1903).

—————— (comp.). *Naval Records of the American Revolution, 1775-1788* (Washington, 1906).

Linn, John Blair (comp.). *Pennsylvania Archives,* Second Series, 19 vols. (Harrisburg, 1879).

Marine Society of the City of New York, Membership List (New York, 1913).

- *Archives of Maryland,* 18 vols. (Baltimore, 1897).

Montgomery, Thomas L. (comp.). *Pennsylvania Archives,* Fifth Series, 8 vols. (Harrisburg, 1906).

Names of Persons for whom Marriage Licenses were issued by the Secretary of the Province of New York, Previous to 1784 (Albany, 1860).

O'Callaghan, E. B. (ed.). *Documents Relative to the Colonial History of the State of New York . . .*, 11 vols. (Albany, 1856-61).

Pelletreau, William S. (ed.). *Abstracts of Wills on File in the Surrogate's Office, City of New York* (New York, 1895-1906).

Purple, Samuel S. (ed.). *Records of the Reformed Dutch Church in New Amsterdam and New York, Marriages from 11 December, 1639 to 26 August, 1801* (New York, 1890).

Reed, G. E. (comp.). *Pennsylvania Archives*, Fourth Series, 14 vols. (Harrisburg, 1900).

Stevens, B. F. (comp.). *Facsimiles of Manuscripts in European Archives Relating to America, 1773-83*, 24 vols. (London, 1889-95).

Stryker, William S. (comp.). *New Jersey Men in the Revolution* (Trenton, 1872).

Wharton, Francis (ed.). *The Revolutionary Diplomatic Correspondence of the United States*, 6 vols. (Washington, 1889).

Wright, Tobias Alexander (ed.). *Baptisms from 1731 to 1800 in the Reformed Dutch Church, New York*, 3 vols. (New York 1900-1902).

Biographies and General Works of History

Abbot, Willis J. *The Naval History of the United States* (New York, 1886).

Abbott, Wilbur C. *New York in the American Revolution* (New York, 1929).

Adams, W. F. *A Few Facts in Connection with the "Life of Commodore Joshua Barney."* Pamphlet (Springfield, Mass., 1910).

Allen, Gardner W. *A Naval History of the American Revolution* (Cambridge, 1913).

Barney, Mary. *Biographical Memoir of the Late Commodore Joshua Barney* (Boston, 1832).

The Clarksons of New York (New York, privately printed, 1876).

Clark, Thomas. *Sketches of the Naval History of the United States*, 2 vols. (Philadelphia, 1813).

Cooper, J. Fenimore. *The History of the Navy of the United States of America*, 4 vols. (Philadelphia, 1839).

Dandridge, Danske. *American Prisoners of the Revolution* (Charlottesville, Va., 1911).

Emmons, George P. *A Statistical History of the Navy of the United States* (Washington, 1850).

Footner, Hulburt. *Sailor of Fortune, The Life and Adventures of Commodore Barney, U.S.N.* (New York, 1940).

Greene, Francis Vinton. *The Revolutionary War and the Military Policy of the United States* (New York, 1911).

Hale, Edward Everett, and E. E. Hale, Jr. *Franklin in France,* 2 vols. (Boston, 1887).

Hall, John and Samuel Clarkson. *Memoirs of Matthew Clarkson of Philadelphia, 1735-1800, and of His Brother Gerardus Clarkson, 1737-1790* (Philadelphia, 1890).

Harbeck, Charles T. *A Contribution to the Bibliography of the History of the United States Navy* (Cambridge, 1906).

Howard, James L. *Seth Harding, Mariner* (New Haven, 1930).

James, W. M. *The British Navy in Adversity* (London, 1926).

Keim, De B. Randolph. *Rochambeau* (Washington, 1907).

Knox, Dudley W. *A History of the United States Navy* (New York, 1936).

Leach, Frank Willing. *The Clarkson Family* (Philadelphia, 1912).

Lee, Richard Henry. *Life of Arthur Lee* (Boston, 1829).

Livingston, Edwin Brockholst. *The Livingstons of Livingston Manor* (New York, 1910).

Maclay, Edgar Stanton. *A History of the United States Navy from 1775 to 1894,* 4 vols. (New York, 1895).

—— *A History of American Privateers* (New York, 1899).

Mackenzie, Charles. *Notes on Haiti* (London, 1830).

Mahan, A. T. *The Influence of Sea Power upon History* (Boston, 1894).

Miller, John C. *Origins of the American Revolution* (New York, 1943).

Neeser, Robert Wilder. *Statistical and Chronological History of the United States Navy,* 1775-1907 (New York, 1909).

Paine, Ralph D. *Joshua Barney, a Forgotten Hero of Blue Water* (New York, 1924).

Parliamentary History (London, 1813).

Paullin, Charles Oscar. *The Navy of the American Revolution* (Chicago, 1906).

Perkins, James Breck. *France in the American Revolution* (Boston, 1911).

Pratt, Fletcher. *The Navy, A History* (New York, 1938).

Sedgwick, Theodore, Jr. *A Memoir of the Life of William Livingston* (New York, 1833).

Spears, John R. *The History of Our Navy,* 4 vols. (New York, 1897).

Stryker, William S. *The Battles of Trenton and Princeton* (Cambridge, 1898).

Van Dyke, John C. *The Raritan, Notes on a River and a Family* (New Brunswick, 1915).

Westcott, Allan and Carroll S. Alden. *The United States Navy, A History* (Philadelphia, 1943).

Williams, Gomer. *History of the Liverpool Privateers and Letters of Marque* (London, 1897).

Youngs, Selah, Jr. *Youngs Family* (New York, 1907).

Printed Diaries and Collections of Letters

Adams, Charles Francis (ed.). *The Works of John Adams,* 10 vols. (Boston, 1851-66).

Aiken, W. B. *Beekman and Van Dyke Genealogies* (New York, 1912).

Ballagh, James Curtis (ed.). *Letters of Richard Henry Lee,* 2 vols. (New York, 1914).

Barck, Dorothy C. (ed.). *Letter Books and Order Book of Admiral Lord Rodney,* 2 vols. in *Collections* of the New-York Historical Society (1932, 1933).

Bates, Albert C. (ed.). *The Deane Papers* (Hartford, 1930).

Chase, Eugene Parker (trans.). *Our Revolutionary Forefathers. The Letters of François, Marquis de Barbé Marbois, 1779-1785* (New York, 1929).

Mill Prison Diary of William Widger of Marblehead in *Historical Collections* of the Essex Institute.

Diary of Frederick Mackenzie, 2 vols. (Cambridge, 1929, 1930).

Duane, William (ed.). *Extracts from the Diary of Christopher Marshall* (Albany, 1877).

Fitzpatrick, J. C. (ed.). *The Writings of George Washington from the original source material,* 30 vols. (Washington, 1931-33).

Ford, Worthington Chauncey (ed.). *Warren-Adams Letters, 1743-1814 . . . ,* 2 vols. (Boston, 1917, 1925).

Fortescue, Sir John (ed.). *The Correspondence of King George the Third,* 4 vols. (London, 1928).

Isham, Charles (ed.). *The Deane Papers,* 5 vols. (New York, 1887-91).

Johnston, Henry P. (comp.). *The Correspondence and Public Papers of John Jay* (New York, 1890).

[Elias Boudinot] Journal, *or Historical Recollections of American Events During the Revolutionary War* (Philadelphia, 1894).

"Journal of Lieutenant, later Rear Admiral Bartholomew James, R.N." in Naval Records Society *Collections* (London, 1896).

Massachusetts Historical Society Collections. *The Trumbull Papers,* 3 vols. (New York, 1900-1903).

Neeser, Robert Wilder (ed.). *Despatches of Molyneux Shuldham* (New York, 1913).

Paullin, Charles Oscar (ed.). *The Out-Letters of the Continental Marine Committee and Board of Admiralty, 1776-1780,* 2 vols. (New York, 1913-14).

Papers of William Vernon and the Navy Board in *Publications* of the Rhode Island Historical Society, VIII (Providence, 1901).

Salley, A. S. (ed.). *Journal of the Commissioners of the Navy of South Carolina,* 2 vols. (Columbia, 1912, 1913).

Warner, Peter Roome (comp.). *Descendants of Peter Willemse Roome* (New York, 1883).

Periodicals

New England Historical and Genealogical Register (Boston): "List of American Prisoners Committed to Old Mill Prison," XIX (1865), 135-150; "Diary of Ezra Green," XXIX (1875), 13-24; "List of American Prisoners in Forton Prison," XXXIII (1876-79), 36-39.

New York Genealogical and Biographical Record (New York): "Records of the Reformed Dutch Church in New York," VII-XXV (1876-97); "Extracts from a Dutch Bible in possession of Warren S. Dey," XXI (1890), 92, 93.

Pennsylvania Magazine of History and Biography (Philadelphia). "Notes and Queries," XIII (1889); "Some Letters of Richard Henry Lee," XXIII (1899); "Notes and Queries," XXVII (1903); "Notes and Queries," XXVIII (1904); Hubertis Cummings (ed.). "Items from the Morris Family Collection of Robert Morris Papers," LXX (1946), 185-208.

John Almon (ed.). *The Remembrancer, or Impartial Repository of Public Events,* 10 vols. (London, 1776-1780).

South Carolina Historical and Genealogical Magazine (Charleston): "Some Letters of Henry Laurens" (1909).

Newspapers

Boston *Gazette* (1775, 1776).
Hartford *Connecticut Courant and Hartford Weekly Intelligencer* (1775-81).
Dunlap's [Philadelphia] *Pennsylvania Packet, or the General Advertiser* (1778-81).
The [Philadelphia] *Freeman's Journal or North American Intelligencer* (1781, 1782).
Boston *Independent Chronicle* (1779, 1780).
Trenton *New Jersey Gazette* (1780, 1781).
London *Gazeteer & Daily Advertiser* (1777).
London *Chronicle* (1772-77).
London *Morning Post.*
New Haven (Conn.) *Journal.*
New York *Gazette and the Weekly Mercury* (1765-81).
New York *Journal or the General Advertiser* (1769-76).
Philadelphia *Pennsylvania Gazette* (1770-81).
Philadelphia *Pennsylvania Journal and Weekly Advertiser* (1770-81).
London *Public Advertiser* (1776, 1777).
Rivington's [New York] *Royal Gazette* (1780, 1781).
Charleston *South Carolina Gazette* (1773).
Charleston *South Carolina Gazette and Country Journal* (1773).
Charleston *South Carolina Royal Gazette* (1780, 1781).
Town's [Philadelphia] *Pennsylvania Evening Post* (1776-78).

Maps and Directories

Thomas Jefferys, "A Chart of the British Channel . . ." (London, 1775)."
"A Map of Philadelphia, 1794."
"Historical Views of Philadelphia, 1800. Printed by William Birch & Son."
MacPherson's Directory for the City and Suburbs of Philadelphia (Philadelphia, 1785).
John Hills, "Plan of the City of Philadelphia," 1796.
Francis White, *The Philadelphia Directory* (Philadelphia, 1785).

Manuscripts and Manuscript Collections

Bank of North American Papers, Historical Society of Pennsylvania, Philadelphia.

John Barry Papers, W. Horace Hepburn Private Collection, Philadelphia.

Thomas Bradford Papers, Historical Society of Pennsylvania, Philadelphia.

British Admiralty Papers, Captains' Letters; Captains' Logs, Class 51; Jamaica Station; Masters' Logs, Class 52; Muster Rolls, Class 36; Secretary, In Letters; Secretary, Miscellanea, Ships' Passes; Public Records Office, London.

British High Court of Admiralty Papers, Prize Papers, New York; Public Records Office, London.

Papers of John Cadwalader, Historical Society of Pennsylvania, Philadelphia.

Committee to Transact Continental Business at Philadelphia Letter Book, Library of Congress, Washington.

Papers of the Continental Congress, Vols. 19, 37, 41, 42, 58, 78, 136, 137, 168, 193, 196, National Archives, Washington, D. C.

Deed Books D, 2, 10, 11, 22, Recorder of Deeds Office, Philadelphia.

Ferdinand J. Dreer Autograph Collection, Historical Society of Pennsylvania, Philadelphia.

Frank M. Etting, Autograph Collection, Historical Society of Pennsylvania, Philadelphia.

Papers of the French Legation in the United States, 1778-94, William S. Mason Collection, Yale University Library, New Haven, Connecticut.

Peter Force Transcripts, Library of Congress, Washington.

Benjamin Franklin Papers, American Philosophical Society, Philadelphia.

Benjamin Franklin Papers, Historical Society of Pennsylvania, Philadelphia.

Benjamin Franklin Papers, University of Pennsylvania Library, Philadelphia.

Benjamin Franklin Papers, William S. Mason Collection, Yale University Library, New Haven, Connecticut.

Simon Gratz Autograph Collection, Catalogued and Uncatalogued Manuscripts, Historical Society of Pennsylvania, Philadelphia.

John Holker Papers, William S. Mason Collection, Yale University Library, New Haven, Connecticut.

188   *THE FIRST SARATOGA*

Joshua Humphreys Papers, M. V. Brewing Private Collection, Cambridge, Maryland.

Joshua Humphreys Papers, Historical Society of Pennsylvania, Philadelphia.

John Paul Jones Papers, Library of Congress, Washington.

Arthur Lee Papers, Harvard University Library, Cambridge, Massachusetts.

Marine Committee and Board of Admiralty Letter Book, Library of Congress, Washington.

Minutes of the Maryland Vice-Admiralty Court, 1776-78, Hall of Records, Annapolis, Maryland.

Papers of Maryland Court of Vice-Admiralty, 1776-89, Hall of Records, Annapolis, Maryland.

Miscellaneous Manuscripts, Historical Society of Pennsylvania.

Robert Morris Diary in the Office of Finance, 1781-84, Library of Congress, Washington.

Robert Morris Papers, Accession 1805, Library of Congress, Washington.

Robert Morris Papers, Historical Society of Pennsylvania, Philadelphia.

Robert Morris Miscellany, New York Historical Society, New York.

Naval Papers Miscellany, Library of Congress, Washington.

Naval Papers Miscellany, New York Historical Society, New York.

Revolutionary Naval Papers, Office of Rolls and Library, Navy Department, Washington.

Navy Board, Eastern Department Letter Book, 1779-82, Library of Congress, Washington.

Diary of George Nelson, 1780-81, Historical Society of Pennsylvania, Philadelphia.

Manuscript Genealogy of the Penfield Family, Louis C. Penfield Estate, Evanston, Illinois.

Admiralty Court Papers of Pennsylvania, Historical Society of Pennsylvania, Philadelphia.

Log of the Continental ship *Ranger,* 1777-80, Office of Rolls and Library, Navy Department, Washington.

Charles Roberts Autograph Collection, Haverford College Library, Haverford, Pennsylvania.

Papers of Vice Admiral George Brydges Rodney, Public Records Office, London.

Ships' Register, 1770-73, Historical Society of Pennsylvania, Philadelphia.

Jared Sparks Manuscripts, Harvard University Library, Cambridge, Massachusetts.

Papers of George Washington, Library of Congress, Washington.

Will Books Q, S, T, U, Register of Wills Office, Philadelphia.

Index

Admiralty Board, *see* Board of Admiralty

Agent of Marine, *see* Robert Morris

Alcide, British ship of the line, 78; pursues and retakes *Providence*, 87, 95

Alexander, Capt. Charles, 2

Alfred, Continental ship, capture of, 17

Alliance, Continental frigate, in France, 26, 31; at Boston, 71, 109

Allison, Lt. Blaney, 86, 119; appointed second lieutenant of *Saratoga*, 35; promoted to first lieutenant, 110; name retained on naval list, 143

Allison, Dr. Francis, 35

Amelia, American schooner, 141

America (American merchant ship), Young's voyages in, 11, 151

America (Continental ship of the line), 29

American Commissioners in France, 15

American Revolution, 1, 37, 93, 133, 137; possible change in course of, 55; gloomy period of, 74; conclusion of, 147

Amphitrite, British frigate, 141

Andrew Doria, Continental brig, 34

Aplin, Capt. Peter, commands *Swift* in retaking ship *Elizabeth*, 100

Arbuthnot, Marriot, 57, 141

Armitage, James, 137

Army, Continental, 3, 43, 56; Young's message halts march of, 15; defeat of, at Camden, 70; dissolution of threatened, 149

Arnold, Benedict, treason of, 74

Babson, Samuel, 137

Bahama Islands, 126, 139

Bailey, Joseph, 111

Bailey, Robert, 38

Baltimore, 14, 18, 33, 135

Barney, Anne, 34

Barney, Lt. Joshua, appointed first lieutenant of *Saratoga*, 33; pay adjustment for, 34, 35; boards *Charming Molly*, 80; ill-treatment of, by British, 96, 102; sent to England, 101; in Mill Prison, 103; exchange of, rejected, 110; escapes, 147

Barney, Mary, 96

Barney, William, 33

Barry, Capt. John, 2, 22, 71

Bayard, Robert, 95

Beaumarchais, Pierre Augustin Caron, 32, 108, 116, 137

Bedford, Gunning, 34

Bellecombe, M. de, governor of Hispaniola, 133, 134, 136, 137, 138

Bickford, Benjamin, 137

Biddle, Capt. Nicholas, 33; death of, in *Randolph*, 2, 17

Bingham, William, 8

Board of Admiralty, 4, 5, 26, 27, 29, 32, 34, 47, 54, 57, 59, 62, 64, 65, 69, 71, 72, 90, 104, 105, 107, 108, 112-16, 135, 143; creation of, 1; asks Congress for funds, 7, 9, 24, 45, 46, 58; appoints Young to new sloop-of-war, 9; names *Saratoga*, 23, 24; objects to building costs, 25; strategy of, impaired, 25, 30; authorized to sell *Saratoga*, 29; selects officers for *Saratoga*, 33; needs money for recruiting, 44, 45; promise of funds to, by Congress, 48; issues cruising orders to

Board of Admiralty (*cont'd.*)
Young, 50-52, 56, 73; sends Young sealed packet, 55; location of office of, 89; concentrates on *Confederacy* and *Saratoga*, 109; receives last muster roll of *Saratoga*, 122
Board of Treasury, 1, 4, 58
Bondfield, John, 16
Bon Homme Richard, Continental ship, 2, 148
Boreas, British frigate, 78
Boston, 7, 15, 26, 31, 32, 48, 71, 102, 107, 108, 143, 147; prizes sent into, 3; shipmasters from, 137
Boston Tea Party, 12
Boston, Continental frigate, 7, 30
Boudinot, Elias, 37
Bourbon, Continental frigate, building in Conn., 2, 25, 26, 29, 31
Bradford, Thomas, Deputy Commissary of Prisoners, 113; Young's prisoners sent to, 92, 122; proposes exchange of Barney, 110
Bristol, England, 11, 151
Brown, John, Secretary of Board of Admiralty, 5, 38, 51, 73, 89, 90; orders by, to Young, 91; reviews unfinished naval business, 143
Brown, Dr. William, 38, 126
Buckskin, Pennsylvania letter of marque schooner, 19
Burgoyne, John, 15, 23
Burroughs, John, 137
Burton, Capt. Hewes, 76
Byng, John, execution of, 17, 18

Camden, battle of, 70
Cape Henlopen, Del., 27, 51, 69, 82, 86, 87, 98, 99, 121
Cape Henry, Va., 75, 78, 87, 141
Cap François, 60, 120, 126, 128, 131, 134-37, 148; Continental frigates ordered to, 32, 56, 108, 116
Carabasse, M., Beaumarchais' agent at Cap François, 32, 56, 60, 108, 116, 135, 137; stores of, depleted by D'Estaing, 133
Castoff, Anthony, 111
Cat, French naval brig, 136
Charleston, S.C., 7, 12, 25, 26, 39, 50,

57, 66, 72, 73, 77, 110, 142, 150, 152; loss of, 30, 74; newspapers of, publish Young's exploits, 124
Charming Molly, British letter of marque ship, captured by Young, 79, 80, 93; sent to Chesapeake Bay, 81, 82, 85; retaken, 94, 96
Charming Sally, Pennsylvania letter of marque ship, 114
Charon, British frigate, 141
Chatham, British ship of the line, 141
Chatham, Pennsylvania letter of marque brig, 142
Chester, Pa., 27, 71, 73, 74, 89, 90, 106, 112, 118
Christophe, Henri, 134
Clarkson, Dr. Gerardus, 43
Clarkson, Matthew, 43
Clarkson, Samuel, midshipman of *Saratoga*, 40, 43, 44, 84, 100
Coates, William, 6
Columbus, Continental ship, burned in Narragansett Bay, 17
Comet, Pennsylvania privateer brig, 114
Comet, South Carolina brig, 110
Commissioners, American, in France, 15
Confederacy, Continental frigate, 5, 8, 30, 43, 45, 48, 51, 53, 59, 69, 70, 105, 109, 112, 116, 118-20, 123, 138, 141; reaches Philadelphia disabled, 26, 27; fouls *Shelaly*, 106; James Nicholson asks transfer to, 107; at Cap François, 131, 133, 135-37; capture of, 143
Congress, *see* Continental Congress
Continental Association, 12
Continental Congress, 1, 2, 5, 8, 12, 14, 17, 18, 28, 45, 47, 53, 54, 57, 58, 64, 71, 105, 108, 110, 115, 116, 143, 147; Joanna Young appeals to, 30, 148, 149; authorizes completion of *Saratoga*, 24, 25; orders frigates to Cap François, 32; adjusts Barney's pay, 34, 35; commissions Van Dyke to marines, 36, 37; orders warrant for advance pay to *Saratoga's* crew, 45; puts frigates under Washington's directions, 48;

sends Henry Laurens to Holland, 50; orders *Saratoga* out under secret orders, 56
Continental currency, 25, 44, 58, 91, 94, 105, 115
Continental shipyard at Southwark, 1, 112; *Saratoga* launched in, 24; *Saratoga* sent to, for repairs, 92
Cornwallis, Lord Charles, 70
Cyclops, British frigate, 78

Daphne, British frigate, 110
Deane, Continental frigate, 30, 45, 48, 50, 53, 59, 73, 75, 105-107, 116, 141; at Boston, 7, 26, 27, 31; in Delaware Bay, 54; supplies for needed, 57; unsuccessful cruise of, with *Trumbull*, 72, 90; sent to Hispaniola, 108; at Cap François, 135-38; arrives at Boston, 143
Delaware Bay, 14, 27, 28, 73, 85, 120
Delaware Capes, 48, 55, 56, 62, 64, 69, 75, 88, 98, 122, 123, 132, 141
Delaware River, 18, 22, 24, 27, 35, 59, 94, 105, 127
Delight, British frigate, 28
D'Estaing, Charles Henri, Count, 133, 135
Des Touches, Charles René, French commodore, 141
Diamond, British letter of marque ship, 136
Dickinson, Pennsylvania row galley, 39
Douglass, British armed brig, taken by Young, 127, 131
Dove, American merchant ship, 109
Drake, British sloop of war, 39

Eaker, Dr. Joseph, 38
Elizabeth, American merchant brig, 12, 152
Elizabeth, British letter of marque ship, capture of, by Young, 82-85, 93; guns of damage *Saratoga*, 92; recapture of, 94, 97-100
Elizabeth, American sloop, retaken by Young, 76, 94; condemnation and sale of, 106, 112
Ellery, William, 17, 24, 48, 58, 71

Faggo, Mary, 39
Faggo, William Brown, 39, 85, 111; dispute of, with Hackett, 97-100; sent to England, 101; writes of ill treatment, 102; escape of, 147
Fair American, Pennsylvania privateer brig, 114; men impressed from, 59; at Cap François, 131, 136; in convoy, 138; arrives at Philadelphia, 142
Favorite, 19, 109
Fisher, Henry, 55, 56, 122
Fisher, Joshua, 114
Fly, Continental sloop, 2
Forbes, James, 24
Foster, Samuel, 137
Franklin, Benjamin, 25, 26, 144, 145
Freeman's Journal, Philadelphia, 146, 147

Galatea, British frigate, 28
Garvin, James, 39, 40
Garvin, John, 38, 39, 111; sent as prizemaster in *Nancy*, 84; taken prisoner, 97; sent to England, 101
Gates, Horatio, defeat of, 70, 74
Geddes, William, 111
General Greene, Pennsylvania privateer ship, 59, 72
General Mifflin, Massachusetts privateer ship, 28
Gerard, Conrad Alexandre, 5, 19, 43
Gerry, Elbridge, 7
Gill, Robert, 80, 110
Goodhue, Joseph, 137
Green, Samuel, 137
Gregg, Archibald, taken in *Douglass*, 127; garbled story of capture of, 128, 129
Grennell, Capt. Thomas, 3
Greyhound, British frigate, 78
Grindley, William, 87
Guadaloupe, British frigate, 75, 78, 87, 95
Guichen, Count de, 55, 60

Hacker, Capt. Hoysteed, 3
Hackett, George, 39
Hackett, John, 39, 111; sent as prizemaster in *Elizabeth*, 84; superceded by Faggo, 85; describes dis-

Hackett, John (*cont'd.*)
　pute with Faggo, 97-100; sent to England, 101
Hallock, Capt. William, 3
Harding, Capt. Seth, commands *Confederacy*, 5; with Young, petitions Board of Admiralty, 44; impresses seamen, 112, 113; conduct of, under fire, 113, 114; to cruise with Young, 116, 118, 119; fails to sail, 120; at Cap François, 133, 138; surrenders *Confederacy* without resistance, 142
Harlem, British sloop-of-war, taken by Young, 22
Havana, 120, 130, 132, 137
Hervey, William, 11
Hinman, Capt. Elisha, 3
Hispaniola, 119, 127, 141, 148
Hobbs, Samuel, 137
Hodge, Capt. John, 3
Holker, Pennsylvania privateer brig, 59
Hopkins, Commodore Esek, 33
Hopkins, Capt. John Burroughs, 3
Hornet, Continental sloop, 34
Hornet, South Carolina brig, 110
Howe, Richard, 15
Humphreys, Joshua, shipbuilder, 2, 9; builds and repairs *Saratoga*, 4, 23, 24, 92, 105, 106

Impertinent, Pennsylvania letter of marque brig, Young's success in, 21, 22; prizes taken by, 157
Independence, Continental sloop, later brig, 11, 13, 14, 93; loss of, on Ocracoke bar, 1, 9, 16, 23, 104; saluted by French fleet, 16; partial muster roll of, 153, 154; prizes taken by, 157
Intrepid, British ship of the line, 78; retakes *Charming Molly*, 96; brutality of captain of, 96
Iris, British frigate, 78, 141; retakes *Saratoga's* last prize, 142; false report of *Saratoga* taken by, 144

Jackways, Capt. Joseph, 131, 132
Jay, John, American minister to Spain, 5, 8, 40, 43; search of, for

Midshipman Livingston, 145, 150
Jay, Sarah, 40, 145
Jersey, British prison ship, 100
Joanna, Pennsylvania letter of marque brigantine, 109
Johnstone, Nicholas, 137
Jones, Capt. John Paul, 2, 39; friend of Young, 15; receives first salute to Stars and Stripes, 16; appeals to Morris in behalf of Joanna Young, 147, 148
Jones, Col. Thomas, 39
Josiah, Capt. James, 2, 3

Keppel, Capt. George, 63, 64
Keppel, British naval brig, engages *Saratoga*, 66-70, 76, 79
Kirkpatrick, Hugh, 111

LaLuzerne, César Anne de, French Minister to America, 5, 28, 47, 48, 52, 59, 138
Lasher, Col. John, 37
Laughton, Capt. John, 121, 122
Laurens, Henry, 50, 51, 53, 65, 94; escorted by *Saratoga* on way to Holland, 54, 55, 57, 61-63; capture of, 64
Lavaud, Bernard, Continental agent at Cap François, 133, 135, 136, 148
Leaming, Thomas, Jr., 114
Lewes, Del., 55, 56, 75, 120, 122, 123
Lewis, Francis, 5, 10, 12, 13, 23, 27, 30-32, 44, 45, 47-49, 51, 52, 56, 58, 59, 64, 69, 72, 75, 104, 105, 107-109, 110, 113, 115, 116, 120, 127; appointed chairman of Board of Admiralty, 1, 2; discouraging picture faced by, 7, 8; plans joint cruises, 25, 28, 30, 71; rebuffed by Congress, 36; reports to Washington on use of Continental vessels, 52, 53; besieges Congress for funds, 57; bad luck of, in naval planning, 60; jubilant over Young's successes, 70, 89, 90; presents woeful picture to Congress, 105; protests excessive bail levied against Young, 115, 116; resigns from Board of Admiralty, 143
Livingston, John Lawrence, mid-

shipman of *Saratoga,* 91, 94; father's advice to, 40-42; reported prisoner in England, 144; reported a captive in Algiers, 149; death of confirmed, 150

Livingston, Kitty, 40, 44; writes Franklin in search of her brother, 144, 145

Livingston, Susan, 40, 91, 144

Livingston, William, Governor of New Jersey, 33; advice of, to son, 40-42; asks Franklin's aid in finding son, 144, 145; imposed upon, 149; death of, 150

London Coffee House, Philadelphia, 122, 128

Lutwidge, Capt. Skeffingham, takes prisoners to England in *Yarmouth,* 101, 102

McClenachan, Blair, 114

McKinley, Allen, 69

McNeill, Capt. Hector, 3

Manley, Capt. John, 3

Marine Committee, 1, 2, 8, 13, 18, 72, 104

Martinique, 13, 14, 43, 93, 113, 133

Mercury, Continental packet, 94; Laurens sail in, for Holland, 50, 53, 54; convoyed by *Saratoga* off Delaware Capes, 61, 62; capture of, 64

Middletown, Conn., 7, 35, 39, 106

Mill Prison, Plymouth, England, 103, 147

Molloy, Capt. Anthony James Pye, 96

Montgomery, Pennsylvania ship of war, 35

Morning Star, Pennsylvania letter of marque brig, 114

Morris, Robert, 14, 19, 150; *Saratoga's* officers report to, 146, 147; asked to adjust Young's accounts, 148

Nancy, British letter of marque brig, 82; taken by Young, 83, 84, 93; retaken by British, 94, 97

Navy Board, Eastern Department, 9, 27, 32

Navy Board, Middle District, 1, 3, 4, 7, 9, 18, 19, 22, 24; without funds, 45, 46; supplies ballast for *Saratoga,* 72, 74; reports repairs needed for *Saratoga,* 90, 92; to provision *Saratoga,* 112, 116

Navy, British, 12; off Sinepuxent, 15; blockading French in Rhode Island, 49, 72, 73; success of, against American privateers, 100; impressments by, 119; takes St. Eustatius, 129; in Leeward Islands, 136; dared by American shipmasters, 137; in engagement with French, 141

Navy, Continental, officers of, 2, 8, 33-35, 101; force of, in northern waters, 7; date of Young's commission in, 13; disaster to, 17; vessels of, to operate with French, 19; reduced by loss of Charleston, 30; joint cruise of planned, 32; frigates of, assigned to French fleet, 47, 48; frigates of, to cruise separately, 72; four ships of, fitting out in Delaware, 105; seamen's uniform in, 111; vessels of, at Cap François, 136-38

Navy, French, co-operation with, 29, 58; fleet of, arrives at Rhode Island, 47; second division of, expected, 53, 59, 116; detachment of, at Santo Domingo, ordered to Rhode Island, 55, 56; in engagement with British, 141

Nesbitt, John Maxwell, 148

New London, Conn., 7, 26, 28, 30

New York City, 1, 11, 26, 42, 57, 66, 68, 70, 72, 74, 78, 80, 94-97, 118, 120-22, 129, 142, 151, 152; treatment of prisoners at, 37; Rodney arrives at, 75; exchange of prisoners from, hampered, 92; newspapers of, tell of Young's successes, 124, 129, 142; horrors of prison ships at, 137

Nicholson, Capt. James, 2, 7, 44, 57, 119; loses *Virginia,* 17, 34; ordered to Philadelphia in *Trumbull,* 26; cruises against orders, 28; encounter of, with *Watt,* 31; letters for

Nicholson, Capt. James (*cont'd.*)
entrusted to Young, 51, 53; evades
escorting Laurens, 54, 55; cruising
with *Deane*, 59, 73, 75, 76; asks
transfer to *Confederacy*, 107, 108;
orders Young to take up deserters, 113

Nicholson, Capt. John, takes command of *Deane*, 109; insubordinate attitude of, 135; at Cap François, 135, 138

Nicholson, Capt. Samuel, 27, 44, 57,
59, 107; relinquishes command of
Deane, 108

Ocracoke Inlet and Bar, N. C., 1, 16,
23

Olney, Capt. Joseph, 3

Orpheus, British frigate, 141, 142

Pearl, British frigate, 141, 142

Pease, Joseph, 137

Penfield, Nathaniel, midshipman of
Saratoga, 40, 43, 95; sent as prizemaster in *Providence*, 86; captured, 95; exchanged, 111; sent as
prizemaster in *Saratoga's* last
prize, 139; retaken, 142; describes
disappearance of *Saratoga*, 140,
146, 150

Penfield, Samuel, 43

Penfield, Samuel, Jr., 43

Penfield, Peter, 43

Pennsylvania Gazette, Philadelphia,
93

Pennsylvania Packet, Philadelphia,
93, 142, 143

Pennsylvania Supreme Executive
Council, 70, 73, 112

Philadelphia, 1, 3, 5-7, 9, 11, 12, 14,
18, 22, 26, 39, 40, 43, 55, 70, 71, 75,
77, 92, 95, 98, 101, 106, 111, 122,
127, 128, 131, 137, 142, 143, 147,
151; heat wave in, 49; newspapers
of laud Young, 93, 128; *Trumbull's* crew deserts at, 108; capture
of merchant fleet from, 121, 122;
false report of Young's sailing
from, 144

Phoenix, British letter of marque
brig, 82-84

Pickles, Capt. William, 61; com-

mands *Mercury* packet, 50; captured by *Vestal*, 63

Picquet, Admiral La Motte, 16

Portsmouth, N. H., 7, 29, 106

Pringle, John, 49, 50, 146

Prisoners of war, American, 37, 92,
100; treatment of described, 102,
103; *Saratoga's* men in prison
ships, 96, 100, 101, 118

Prisoners of war, British, taken by
Young, on second cruise, 81, 84,
87, 88; housed in new Philadelphia jail, 90; landed at Henlopen,
121; and overload gun on *Saratoga*, 134, 135

Prizes, American, *Sarah*, 69; *Elizabeth* (sloop), 76; *Charming Molly*
and *Two Brothers*, 80, 81; *Elizabeth* (ship), and *Nancy*, 83, 84;
Providence, 86; two vessels by
Trumbull and *Deane*, 90; *Resolution*, 120, 121; *Tonyn*, 123-26;
Douglass, 127; *Diamond*, 136; un-
named snow, 139; list of, taken by
Young, 158

Prizes, British, *Charming Molly*,
Elizabeth, *Nancy*, and *Providence* retaken, 95-100; thirteen
privateers taken by Rodney, 100;
Confederacy, taken by *Orpheus*
and *Roebuck*, 141, 142; *Amelia*, 141

Providence, Continental frigate, 3,
7, 30

Providence, Continental sloop, 3

Pyne, Lt. James, 110, 111

Queen of France, Continental ship,
7, 30

Raleigh, British frigate, 78, 96

Raleigh, Continental frigate, 17

Randolph, Continental frigate, 2, 17

Ranger, Continental ship, 7, 30, 39

Ranger, Pennsylvania row galley,
40

Read, James, 9

Read, Capt. Thomas, 2, 35

Reed, Joseph, 69, 73

Reedy Island, 31, 118

Reprisal, Continental ship, 2

Resolution, British privateer ship,
taken by Young, 120, 121; con-

demned and sold at Philadelphia, 122, 124, 128
Restoration, British privateer brig, 76
Ridley, Matthew, 145
Rivington, James, 70, 128, 129
Robinson, Capt. Isaiah, 3
Robinson, Capt. James, 2
Rochambeau, Jean Baptiste, Count de, 28, 137
Roebuck, British frigate, 141, 142
Rhode Island, 49, 141, 144
Rodney, George Brydges, British admiral, brings fleet to New York, 74, 75; sends frigates to scour coast, 77; vessels of retake Young's prizes, 95; captures thirteen American privateers, 100; converts *Jersey* to prison ship, 100, 101; calls American captains "notorious offenders," 102; at St. Lucia, 131; captures St. Eustatius, 136; plunder of retaken in *Diamond,* 136
Roome, Susanna, 42
Royal Gazette, New York, 128, 129
Rutledge, South Carolina galley, 110

Sachem, Continental sloop, 34
St. Augustine, 123, 124, 128
St. Eustatius, 120, 152; taken by Rodney, 129, 130
Saltonstall, Capt. Dudley, 3, 33
Sandy Hook, 73, 75-77, 99
Sarah, British merchant snow, taken by *Saratoga,* 69-71; seamen of, sent to jail, 74; prize money from, at opportune time, 106
Saratoga, American merchant brig, taken at St. Eustatius, 129, 130
Saratoga, Continental sloop-of-war, 7, 30, 46, 64, 70, 73, 78, 87, 89, 90, 91, 95-97, 104, 109, 114; dimensions of, 4; named by Board of Admiralty, 24; launched, 24, 25; to cruise with *Trumbull,* 26, 27; sale of authorized, 29; ready for service, 31; officers selected for, 33-44; crew for recruited, 45; placed under direction of Washington, 48; to convoy packet *Mercury,* 50, 53, 61-63; to bring stores from Cap François, 56; not available for proposed mission, 59, 60; engages *Keppel,* 65-68; takes *Sarah,* 69; begins second cruise, 74; retakes sloop *Elizabeth,* 76; takes *Charming Molly* and *Two Brothers,* 79-81; takes ship *Elizabeth* and *Nancy,* 83-85; retakes *Providence,* 86; returns from successful cruise, 88; officers of praise Young, 94; prizes of retaken, 100, 101; officers of sent to Mill Prison, 103; repair bills for, 106, 107; officer replacements for, 110, 111; to sail for Cap François, 116, 117; off Reedy Island, 118; sails from Delaware, 120; takes *Resolution,* 120, 121; lands prisoners at Cape Henlopen, 122; takes *Tonyn* and *Douglass,* 123-27; newspapers tell of cruise of, 128; falsely reported taken at St. Eustatius, 129, 130; at Cap François, 131, 132, 135; gun bursts on board, 134; takes *Diamond,* 136; takes British snow, 139; disappears at sea, 140; fears for, at Philadelphia, 143, 144; rumors of capture of, 144, 145; Agent of Marine told of loss of, 146; wills of crew members of probated, 146; reported taken by the Algerines, 149
Scott, James, 10
Sebring, Barent, 40, 42
Sebring, Barent, Sr., 42
Semple, William, 6, 49, 50, 109, 146, 148
Shelaly, Pennsylvania letter of marque ship, 106
Shoemaker, Samuel, 6
Sinepuxent Bay, Md., 14, 15, 22
Smith, Joseph, 137, 142
Southwark, 1, 3, 9, 18, 22, 24
Steel, John, 66, 68
Stroson, John, 148
Sturmfelts, George, 147
Swift, British brig, retakes ship *Elizabeth,* 100

Taylor, David, 84
Ternay, Admiral Louis, Chevalier de, 28, 47-49, 71, 73, 75, 141
Terrible, British ship of the line, 78
Thackstone, William, 87; exchanged for Penfield, 111
Thompson, Capt. Thomas, 3
Thorndike, Andrew, 137
Tobago, American merchant brig, 10, 11, 132, 151
Tonyn, British letter of marque ship, taken by *Saratoga*, 123-26; capture of, described to Lewis, 127; carried into Cap François, 131; proceeds from sale of, 133
Torbay, British frigate, 130
Treasury, *see* Board of Treasury
Triton, British frigate, 75, 78, 87, 95
Triumph, British ship of the line, 78
Truite, South Carolina ship, 110
Trumbull, Continental frigate, 30, 31, 45, 48, 51, 53, 54, 73, 109, 116; James Nicholson appointed to, 2; at New London, 7, 26; engages *Watt*, 31; to cruise with *Saratoga*, 50; rigging and stores for, 57; ordered to cruise, 59; cruising with *Deane*, 72, 75, 90; near mutiny on board, 106, 107; desertions from, 107, 108; Young to take up deserters from, 109, 113, 114
Turk's Island, 131, 138
Two Brothers, British letter of marque sloop, 81, 83, 94, 106, 112

Van Dyke, Abraham, 36, 37, 111
Van Dyke, Anna Verkerk, 37
Van Dyke, Jan, 37
Vestal, British frigate, 63, 64
Virginia, Continental frigate, 17, 34
Virginia Capes, 141, 142

Wade, John R., 123, 124, 125
Washington, George, 14, 37, 58, 59, 71, 74; recommends Van Dyke, 36-38; to direct Continental frigates, 48, 52; sends *Saratoga* on mission, 56

Washington, Continental frigate, 35
Wasp, Continental schooner, 34
Watt, British letter of marque ship, 31
West, William, 89
West Florida, Continental sloop, 44, 45, 50
West Indies, 17, 57, 108, 116, 135
Wharton, John, 9
Whipple, Capt. Abraham, 3
Wickes, Capt. Lambert, 3, 33
Will, William, 114, 115, 132, 143
Willing & Morris wharf, Philadelphia, 70, 128
Winder, William, 9

Yarmouth, British ship of the line, 101-103, 147
York, Pa., 17
Young, Joanna, 147; appeals for widow's half-pay, 10, 148, 149; furnishes Laurel street home, 19-21; as executrix of husband's will, 50; farewell of, to husband, 116, 117; fears of, 143; probates husband's will, 146; death of, 150
Young, Capt. John, of the Continental navy, 4, 7, 8, 18, 23, 27, 31, 54, 59, 72, 74, 90, 91, 97, 112; exonerated in loss of *Independence*, 1; home of, 3, 18, 109; appointed to *Saratoga*, 9; early naval experiences of, 10, 13, 15, 19, 21; shares with Jones in first salute to Stars and Stripes, 16; loses *Independence* on Ocracoke bar, 17; commands *Buckskin*, 19; in command of *Impertinent*, 21, 22; recommends heavier guns for *Saratoga*, 25; reassured by Lewis, 29; selects officers, 33-39; appeals for pay increase for crew, 44, 45; makes will, 49, 50; to escort packet *Mercury*, 51, 55; finds *Saratoga* a sluggish sailer, 61, 62; operating under conflicting orders, 64, 65; engages *Keppel*, 66-68; returns from first cruise with *Sarah*, 71; sailing orders for second cruise, 73; second cruise of,

74-88; retakes sloop *Elizabeth*, 76; takes *Charming Molly* and *Two Brothers*, 79-81; takes *Nancy* and ship *Elizabeth*, 83-85; retakes *Providence*, 86; report of, to Board of Admiralty, 89; called a gallant captain, 93; anxiety of, for prizes, 94; Lewis elated by success of, 104; shipping ventures of, with Semple, 109; replaces captured officers, 109; policing river for deserters, 113, 114; arrested under excessive bail by high sheriff, 114, 115; ordered to sail for Hispaniola, 116; sails from Philadelphia, 117; third cruise of, 118-30; takes *Resolution*, 120, 121; fights greatest battle with *Tonyn*, 123-26; takes *Douglass*, 127; writes Lewis of capture of *Tonyn*, 127; in Tory press, 129; arrives at Cap François, 131, 132-34; in joint cruise with *Confederacy, Deane*, and *Cat*, 136; sails from Cap François on last cruise, 137, 138; and capture of British snow, 139; disappears with *Saratoga*, 140; last prize of retaken, 142; letters for, in Philadelphia postoffice, 143; erroneously reported killed in action, 144; false report of letter from, 144; epitaph of, written by newspaper, 146, 147; services of, described to Congress, 148; widow of, refused half-pay, 149

Young, Samuel, 87

Young, Walter, commands *Alcide*, 87; libels against *Providence*, 95